D1860720

A TEXTUAL STUDY OF THE APU TRILOGY

A TEXTUAL STUDY OF THE APU TRILOGY

SATISH BAHADUR
SHYAMALA VANARASE

VANI PRAKASHAN

VANI PRAKASHAN

4695, 21-A, Daryaganj, New Delhi 110 002

Branch

Ashok Rajpath, Patna 800 004

Phone : +91 11 23273167 Fax : +91 11 23275710

www.vaniprakashan.in
vaniprakashan@gmail.com

A TEXTUAL STUDY OF THE APU TRILOGY
by Satish Bahadur/Shyamala Vanarase
Edited by Rakesh Manjul

ISBN : 978-93-5000-428-9
Text Book/Cinema

First Edition

Price : ₹ 295

Printed at Om Offset Platemaking, Delhi 110 093

Vani Prakashan's logo is a creation of the strokes from M.F. Husain

CONTENTS

PERSONAL NOTE

I was Professor of Film Appreciation at Film and Television Institute of India in its early decades from 1963 to 1983. Earlier, from 1959 to 1963, I had run two film societies in Agra, one in the university and the other in the city. Also, I had done some work on the structure and meaning of Indian films for UNESCO study project on the Image of the Film Hero in 17 Cultures.

In my very early years serious thinking on a specific film would involve identifying what one liked in the film, hoping that this would help critical understanding of the film. However, any method involving personal preference would not convince serious students in a film society core or those learning film making at the Film Institute.

Judgement about a film had to be based on objective evidence from within the film. A method of film analysis in terms of its own parts had to be developed, as also a supporting frame of aesthetic concepts. This method should reveal how a work of art in the film medium is put together as a whole. We had to distinguish a work of Art from a film which was organised skillfully as a product for mass consumption by threading entertainment elements along a narrative line of familiar stereotypes.

The classics were convenient material for teaching film structure for students at the Film Institute. Sergei Eisenstein's analysis of the macrostructure of *The Battleship Potemkin* was readily available, as also hints for understanding the microstructural levels. Several other film classics, including some shorts, were also analysed as teaching material in Film Appreciation classes. To recall a small sample list which emerged over the years of my analytical teaching: *Bicycle Thieves* (Italy, de Sica), *Rashomon* (Japan, Kurosawa) *Wild Strawberries* (Sweden, Bergman), *Citizen Kane* (U.S.A., Welles), *La Dolce Vita* (Italy, Federico Fellini), *Hiroshima, Mon Amour* (France , Alain Resnais). Amongst short films we had *Night Mail* (U.K., Harry Watt & Basil Wright), *Glass*

(Netherlands, Bert Haanstra), *Delta Phase One* (Netherlands, Bert Haanstra), *Big City Blues* (Netherlands, Charles van der Linden), *Love Thy Neighbour* (Canada, Norman McLaren), *Happy Anniversary* (France, Pierre Etaix & Jean-Claude Carriere) and *Panchthupi, a Village in West Bengal* (India, Hari Dasgupta).

Satyajit Ray's *Pather Panchali* clearly belonged to the category of a work of Art, and it was tried out as text material in many courses. As classroom texts, *Pather Panchali* (Song of the Road, 1955), and the other two films of the Trilogy which continue the Apu story, *Aparajito* (The Unvanquished, 1956) and *Apur Sansar* (The World of Apu, 1959), had distinct advantage for Indian students. The fiction of the Apu Trilogy deals with processes of Indian life and society, which could easily be followed after the Bengali language dialogue had been translated adequately, and some cultural and historical specifics of the films are understood by students. The details of the film are relatively easy to grasp as a first exercise. The analysis of *Pather Panchali* was also used in extension programmes in cities all over India.

In retrospect, while teaching Film Appreciation at the Film Institute, two compelling reasons emerged why analytical work should be done on the basis of international classics of the Cinema. One reason was technical, the second, which was related to the technical reason, a moral one.

First, the technical reason. An art work is an organic Whole in which the constituent elements are logically related to each other, and also to the web of themes. Thus, a classic has no redundant elements which exist for their own sake. Hence, it is easy to comprehend the relationship between structure and meaning in a work of Art. **A work of Art is**, in this sense, **easier teaching and learning material.**

The moral reason was the fact that the Film Institute was set up to train students for the production of the **new** Indian film. Hence the teaching had also to be oriented with examples of the artistic cinema, as distinct from the mass entertainment film. **The value problem with the entertainment film is that it trivialises, even falsifies the very social issues in the plot by converting them for mass entertainment** through the use of devices like song and dance and stereotypes, and good looking actors, attractive locations and high end consumer goods as properties. Hence the entertainment film was unsuitable teaching material in the moral sense.

My main teaching work was with students of the Film Institute. However, we were also doing considerable **extension teaching** in short courses in Film Appreciation for select groups of film enthusiasts. After 1967 we had begun a one month residential course at Pune during the summer vacation which has attracted participants from all over the country. The course of 2009 was the thirty fifth in this series. I also went out to teach courses of five to ten days duration anywhere in the country for a host film society or educational institution, literally from Rajkot to Imphal and Chandigarh to Trivandrum. The presentation and analysis of classic films in the courses has been done for a very wide range of persons.

The analysis of classics was done with the objective of presenting the students a method for exploring any film. The detailed textual analysis of a film classic is exacting work, but is worth the effort since it reveals the devices which make the film an expressive form. Many sensitive persons who watch classic films receive the impact of the film alright but find it difficult to identify what actually creates the richness of the film experience. This detailed analysis will help notice the devices which give depth to film composition.

I recall an occasion when I checked with Satyajit Ray my method of analysing *Pather Panchali*. His response, in effect, was : **This is exactly what he had done, though this is not the way he had done it.** Satyajit elaborated that he conceived the emerging form of the film in musical terms. Thus, he handled structure, symmetry, contrast, balance, tone, overtone (and the like) in the film as if it was a musical composition. The connection can be made now. **Music is the most abstract of all the Arts. That is why all Arts (Film included) aspire to the condition of Music.**

Shyamala Vanarase, my co-author, is a psychologist, HRD consultant and art critic, and she has taught numerous Film Appreciation extension courses with me and also with others. My interaction with her has evolved the method of presenting the material here. She has several publications on her professional subjects. A series of articles on the films of Satyajit Ray has already been published by her. She has a forthcoming Marathi book on the Ray films as reflection of the psycho-social changes in Indian society.

Prachi Dublay, a vocalist, has generously advised with problems of music in the films. My son **Apurva**, 47, named in honour of the Trilogy, has helped with stills and with computer problems. **Harshwardhan Gupta**, **S.Theodore Baskaran** and **Sushama Datar** have very kindly read the manuscript with approval and comments. **Samik Banerji** has helped in numerous ways.

We are grateful to **Sandip Ray** for permission to use stills from the films.

Rakesh Manjul has contributed in varied ways during the production of the book.

Pune

15th Dec., 2009

– Satish Bahadur

INTRODUCTION

This is a study of the three films of Satyajit Ray: **Pather Panchali** (Song of the Road, 1955), **Aparajito** (The Unvanquished, 1956) and **Apur Sansar** (The World of Apu, 1959) which are popularly known as **The Apu Trilogy. We focus on the design of the narrative presented by the film maker on the screen. In this sense it is a study of the text of films, the warp and woof of the elements which hold the films together. All other aspects of the films are outside the frame of our study, not because they are not important, but simply because they are outside our frame.** Thus, we do not refer to the biographical details of Satyajit Ray and the vast range of his other films, or to the production details of the Trilogy, or to problems of adaptation from the novel, and numerous such aspects. **We have firmly confined ourselves to the study of text of the films.**

Now I describe **the method for the actual teaching of analysis of the classics** for students learning film making. I am numbering the different stages in the progression of teaching to keep my statement clear. **(1) At the first stage** some specially written progamme notes on the film are given, one copy for each student. These notes contain brief introduction to the production credits of the film, as also the social history of the background to the plot. Any cultural complications of the characters are also briefly explained. The main body of these notes contains the macrostructure of the film, which, in effect, is the progression of the film in terms of large segments of the plot. If the script of the film exists as a book in print, the students are encouraged to read it independently. **(2) The second stage** is the first projection of the film. It is done with a brief introduction by me, mainly drawing attention to the programme notes circulated earlier. The film is projected continuously. It is followed by a very brief period in which some first reactions are noted. Students are asked to read the macrostructure carefully. Now that they have seen the film, it should make more sense. **(3) The third stage.** The next day, the film is projected again with some lights on at the back of the hall, which enables students to maintain a mental distance from the screen and see the visual image as a cinematographic image and to hear the sounds as audioimages. During the projection I am with a portable mike, my voice audible above the slightly lowered sound volume of the film.The film is run sequence to sequence, and while it is running I make observations on the visual composition of shots, the design of sound and significant editing devices. The purpose is to draw attention to the microstructural details of the film. At the end of a sequence, the projection would be halted, the hall lights switched on, and I would work on the blackboard handling questions and giving further explanations. If I felt that the microdetails of audio-visual compositions had not quite got across to students in one screening, I would project the sequence again, and give more pointed attention to whatever needed further emphasis. A run of the visuals of a scene **without sound** would enable the visuals to be seen with pointed attention, also draw attention to the sounds which are missing. Likewise, a run of the sound track with **the visuals switched off** would draw pointed attention to the multiplicity of sound elements and how they get related to the missing visuals. I am talking of the days of 16 mm or 35 mm film when we needed careful coordination with the film projectionist. Now with the film on DVD, the teacher himself can control the projection.

During such analytical exercises the students have to be reminded all the time that **we are not watching the film: we are studying it.** In any group there would always be some students who would protest against killing the film, as if we are plucking the wings off a beautiful butterfly. Analysis is not killing, it is activating the mind to discover what makes the film a living thing. It is the carefully selected and arranged audiovisual details which lend depth to the film composition and make it a rich experience.

The material for this book has emerged from actual teaching situations. Hence the writing style occasionally uses a free flowing conversational method with a classroom flavour.

This is a teacher's book written by teachers for students and of course, for other teachers. A teacher's book is different from a critic's book and also a scholar's book. A critic's book uses a style for comfortable, pleasurable reading even while making profound observations on a film. It is addressed to a wide readership across the book reading community, national and international. A scholar's book is research based and is meant primarily for other research workers the world over, as also for teachers who could selectively use the material in the book for appropriate use with students. Most often students find a scholar's book high above them, and appropriately so.

A teacher's book is shaped as a learning tool. It is not designed for smooth reading. In actual fact, it is dense writing and needs attentive, unhurried reading. Anything which needs emphasis is printed in bold type to draw attention to the importance of what is in bold type. Likewise, when the macrostructure of a film is being analysed the importance of the Part-Whole Relationship is re-emphasised by separating the description of the parts by inserting appropriate headings for the parts. Also, there are novel feaures in the indexes. There are no references to other books or journals because this teacher's book does not use any authority other than the three films. The only authority quoted once in this book is Satyajit Ray himself.

Also, we made some assumptions about the reader when deciding the level of this book. This is a book on the Apu Trilogy and we assume that our reader has seen the films, and also has access to the films for crosschecking the detailed relationships presented in the book. This is a fair assumption about a serious student of cinema since discs of all the three films of the Trilogy with English subtitles are readily available in all major cities in India, also on the internet. For flow of scenes and English translation of dialogues, one could easily use the book Satyajit Ray: *"The Apu Trilogy*", English version based on the original films in Bengali by Shampa Banerji (2003. Seagull Books, 26, Circus Avenue, Kolkata 700-007. Edition:Second).

In writing this text we sometimes use abbreviations for names of films, PP for PATHER PANCHALI, APJT for APARAJITO and AS for APUR SANSAR.

Our concern with design in the film needs constant forward and back references. **Hence a system for numbering of scenes in the film has been devised which needs patient handling, as in all referencing work. THUS APJT 32 WOULD REFER TO SCENE NO. 32 IN INDEX OF SCENES IN APPENDIX.**

The narrative in Satyajit Ray's films is usually simple and easily understood. **However, his statements achieve deep levels through the complexity of audio-visual composition of cinematic images. Ray puts it as follows: "It has been**

my preoccupation to achieve as much density as possible within a superficially simple narrative structure". Artists keep on searching ways to articulate the inarticulable through compositional devices. The point about such **density of expression** is illustrated here with **two detailed examples.**

The sequence is covered in **PP 30-32.** Sarbojaya is with the last handfuls of grain to feed the children. Reluctantly she picks up the coin loaned by Nilmoni's Wife, when Apu comes in shouting with a letter. She moves forward from a medium closeup to a closeup, holding the letter while the husband's voice reads out what he has written of how after all these delays he is coming home now. A broad smile lights up her face, which dissolves into ripples on the surface of the pond.

A sitar tune flexes along with the movement of the

visuals. The visual details are not mere pretty-to-look-at simultaneous events as they progress from the suddenly stirred woman to the ripples on the water surface, to insects gliding along, freely flying around a twig, and floating leaves and a flower, more insects, more ripples, on to a kitten frisking around a patient female dog. The camera moves past the caged bird, past the distant closed door which will be opened by the husband when he comes home as it goes down to a lying-down Sarbojaya fanning herself, the mature sensuous woman whose exuberance of expectation is caged in by the restraint of waiting, and further down to Durga, the on-the-verge woman decorating herself and praying for maturity. The background

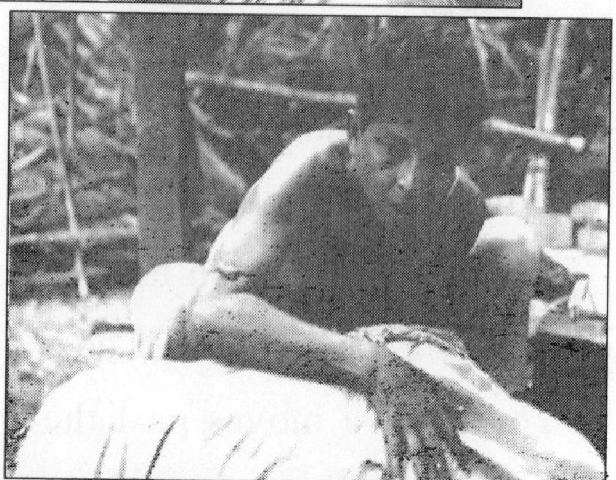

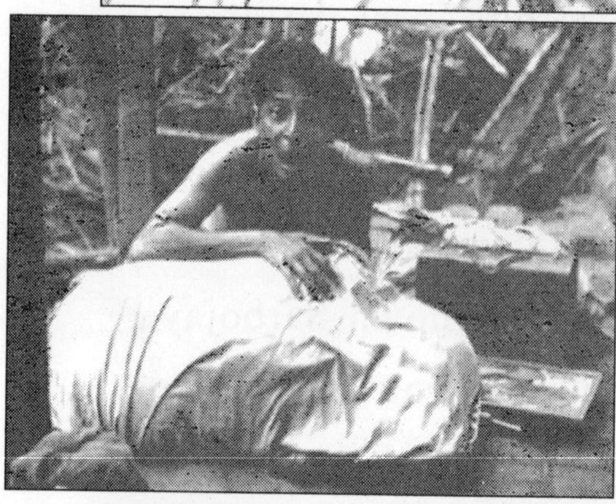

sitar piece ends as Durga settles down to the ritual for a good husband.

This complex filmic composition traces the form of a nuance of feeling which is otherwise inarticulable. This is the precise function of composition : to make the life of feeling articulable by presenting equivalent structures in the material frame of the film language.

In the second example, a musical piece links very distant situations, one in *Pather Panchali* and the other in *Apur Sansar*. In PP 36, when Sarbojaya breaks down telling Harihar of Durga's death, the sound of her weeping is replaced by a music tune in the higher reaches of Raga Patdeep; let us name it Mother's Wail. (For the musical shape of Mother's Wail refer to Index on Music). Mother's Wail covers Harihar as he shares his sudden grief with Sarbojaya in physical together-ness, and the music

also goes on to Apu, he has heard the father cry, and he hesitates before moving towards the house.

In *Apur Sansar* (AS-81) a small segment of Mother's Wail is used again in the conciliation scene between Kajal and Apu. Apu had failed several intensive attempts to connect with his six year old son Kajal. He has given up, and is finally leaving, going, moving away along the river bank. At a distance Kajal stands tensed up expectantly, keeps on gazing at the going away Apu. Apu senses all this and halts, turns around and asks Kajal if he wants to say something. In a short verbal interchange, Kajal accepts Apu as "a friend" who will take him to "his father" in Calcutta.

In the meanwhile, Grandfather has also come in the distance calling out affectionately for Kajal. Apu beckons Kajal to come to him assuring him that Grandfather would not know. As Kajal runs towards Apu in this moment of acceptance, a high snippet of Mother's Wail covers Apu's face and Kajal's short run towards him (see Index on Music). Apu and Kajal make physical contact as Apu picks up Kajal and they move away from Grandfather. Apu has Kajal on his shoulders and the very triumphant title music (see Index on Music) takes over as we move to the end of the film.

This short moment of Kajal's run is also the culmination of Apu's six year long silent wail over Aparna's death. Aparna's death had deprived Kajal of his mother and also of his father, and this was the source of Kajal's unhappiness. **Mother's Wail seems to validate two extreme contrasts of family togetherness. In Durga's death, the family loses the darling daughter. In Kajal's acceptance of Apu, the son finds his lost father. The device of Mother's Wail covers both intense grief and intense joy. It is probably true that intense joy and intense grief are of one piece.** This example will be referred to again later when we deal with music.

An artist creates an underpinning layer of feeling beneath the narrative structure. A probe into these underpinning layers of feeling will help in a mature understanding of the film. The Trilogy has density of this kind all the way through all the films. We will constantly attempt to probe this density as we study the narrative structure of the films.

●●

Chapter 1

LOGIC OF FILM ANALYSIS

Film is **an image**. An image is **a virtual object** which exists for perception only. The film image is multilayered. The need to analyse films emerges from the need to discuss individual films. Works of film art always leave you with a feeling that there is more to it than what you catch in the first viewing.

Exploration of the film involves two kinds of probe (i) identifying the underpinning layers of feeling beneath the narrative structure, and (ii) identifying the elements of design and the binding principles which provide rhythm to the film. **This two-level method of analysis uses some <u>ideas about the film medium</u> which are relevant for the systematic understanding of any film.**

<u>These ideas about the film medium</u> are presented here under four convenient **headings** :(i) Nature of Film Image (ii) Whole-Part Relationship in Film Image (iii) Structure and Function of Film Image, and (iv) Design in Film.

Nature of Film Image

An image is a virtual object which exists for perception only. The concept of **virtual object** emerged when scientists tried to understand the nature of the visual image formed by a plane mirror. The image of a candle in front of a plane mirror was "there", you could see it but you could not touch it, you could not receive it on a surface. **The image existed for perception only** for seeing. It was **<u>a virtual object</u>**.

Nature provided several examples of such virtual objects, like the rainbow which looks like a multicoloured path in the sky. However, there is no path in the sky. The rainbow is a virtual image caused by the interaction of rays of light with raindrops. Likewise, reflections in the surface of a water pool are virtual objects.

Then, it was realised that human beings had always been making such virtual objects, like in a painting you see a personage, or trees or fruit. You could see the person, but you could not shake hands with him, you could not climb that tree, nor could you eat that fruit. **They were virtual objects; they were images, which existed for perception only.** Likewise, human beings made images in several media, dance, song, theatre, novel, story, poem, photograph, film…add more. Some visual images looked real, but were not real; they were virtual.

There were numerous mythical stories about **a virtual object being confused for a real object**, like the Chinese story of the painter whose painting of a forest was so realistic that he walked into it and got lost. Also the Greek legend of Pygmalion who sculpted a woman in stone and fell in love with it and pined for her so much that the Gods were kind and changed the stone into a flesh and blood woman.

A favourite story, apocryphal of course, is of Picasso, the painter who lived like a recluse in a detached villa somewhere on the French seaside. An American soldier stealthily broke into the villa and had a good leisurely look at the paintings. When he was going away, the Master hailed him back. "Hey, Joe, come back. Have a drink before you go." Thus relaxed, Picasso asked him: "Tell me, what do you think of my paintings?" The young man decided to be honest: "They are alright, but I find them unrealistic…" Picasso nodded in agreement. When the young man was just about to go out from the front gate of the villa, the Master hailed him back again. "Tell me, Joe, do you have a girl friend back home?" Readily, Joe took out of his wallet a photograph of the girl friend back home. The Master took the photograph in his hand: "Just three inches high, that's a very tiny woman. Tell me, Joe, how do you make love to her?"

Popular Urdu poetry has the same concept expressed is some lines. **Tasveer teyree dil meraa bahlaa na sakeygee** (your picture can no longer continue to be comforting me). Another line which sort-of translates Picasso : **Jo baat tujh meyn hai, teree tasveer meyn naheen** (what you have in you is not there in your picture.) And yet another poet lifts this concept of the image to create an event of a philosopical plane : **Woh mil gayey to apnaa hi dhokaa hua hameyn / Aaeena aaj dekh key nikaley thay ghar sey hum.** (When I happened to run into him today by mere chance, I got the illusion of meeting myself. I had indeed preened myself in a mirror before going out of my house.)

Photographic realism is a basic property of film image. It goes back to 1895, to the very origin, to the Lumiere Cinematographe which was hailed by the press headline: "It's like life!" It was suggested that the name cinema (based on kinema, kino, movement) was not adequate, more appropriate names for the new gadgetry could be biograph and vitagraph (based on bio and vita, life itself).

Some thirty years later when the realism of sound was added to silent moving-photographic visuals you had the sound film, which was even more realistic since you could see the characters on screen moving around and also hear them speak.

The screen image of Manoj Kumar walking and singing on the beach looks as if Manoj Kumar himself is walking and singing on the beach in front of me.

The film medium directly involves the **two important sense organs of the spectator, the eye and the ear**. The spectator is put in a dark hall where he can see and hear only what is on the screen. On the screen is seen and heard what the camera "saw" and the mike "heard" when the film was made. In effect, the film works as if the spectator's eye is behind the camera and he sees on the screen what the camera "saw"when the film was made. Likewise, his ear is behind the mike and he hears what the mike "heard" when the film was made. When the film was shot, the camera and the mike were at the beach, in the same space as the actor. The spectator therefore also gets the feeling of **"being in the same space"**, on the beach with Manoj Kumar. Thus, **while the spectator is in his chair watching the film in a dark cinema house, he gets the feeling that he is also himself on the beach where Manoj Kumar is walking and singing.**

The illusion that the spectator is "in" the same space as the actor is a special property of the big screen image in a cinema house. For the small sized TV or video image, the spectator is always aware of the space of his room where he sits while seeing-hearing the image on the small screen on the table in front of him, and almost never does the TV spectator the illusion of being "there" in the same space as the screen event. **This is the main difference between the big screen image and the small screen image.** The illusion of being "in" the same space again goes back to a Lumiere screening when some spectators bolted from their seats to the safety of side walls when the train entering the station moved towards them.

The language of cinema is, as if, built into the human system. Without any knowledge of camera or sound or editing, anyone sees the image on the big screen in a cinema house, or on the small TV screen and understands it.When you cut from a long shot of a person to a medium shot, there is a shift of ten feet in your viewing position, but it does not give any jerk, because the film is doing the equivalent of what we do in life: as we get more interested in the person we see with more close attention, without changing our position. From a medium we shift to a close up on the face, it is just a shift of your attention process which is being reproduced by the shot taking and editing.

In effect, **editing follows four processes which are also the processes with which the mind works**. **(i)** If the shots are placed in chronological order, the mind joins them and **makes sense of the narrative**. **(ii)** If two elements which are otherwise unrelated are edited together **the mind makes a judgement** about their relationship. **(iii)** If numerous details about a subject are put together, the mind takes them in and **browses**. **(iv)** If shots are edited together in free association, the mind takes them in as in dreaming, **in day dreaming**. There are many more processes. The human mind is highly versatile: the shots can be in any other order, and the mind will make some sense of the editing construction.

Let us plan filming a scene between Boy (B) and Girl (G) using an elementary story situation. I am supplementing this verbal description of the exercise with sketches, deliberately maintaining the rough and ready drawing style used by me on the blackboard which I used when teaching in a classroom. G is waiting for B in a garden. B comes. B and G talk to each other, then they part. For filming, you need the camera-mike, the actors playing B and G and the garden location. The tools of film making are essential for making a film. Without the camera and the mike you cannot make an inch of film. The camera-mike is the eye-ear of the film maker, it is also the eye-ear of the spectator. Let X be the name of the camera-mike, a bodyless, invisible presence. Thus, in film you tell the B and G story as if it is happening between B and G and X, whose role will change with every change in the camera-mike position.

Let's start. An extreme long shot on G, under a tree in this lonely garden. X in extreme distance. Who's she? What is she doing in this lonely garden? Curiosity aroused, we cut to a medium shot with X at a fair distance noticing that G is distressed. Cut to close shot and further to close up when X can see details of tears in her eyes and even hear the song which B and G sang together earlier. X is now acting as an observer in the scene with varying intimacy, from the very distant to the

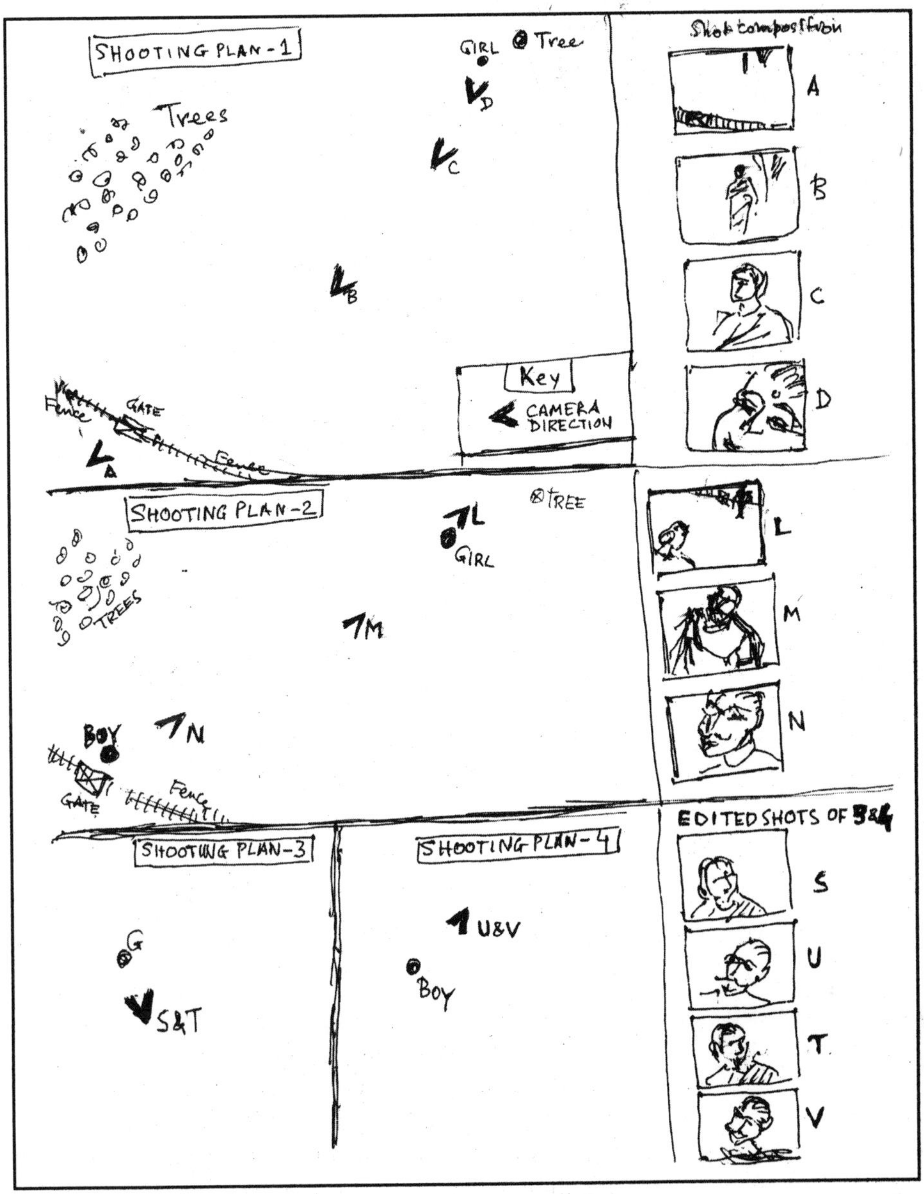

very intimate, even to the extent of hearing what is going on in G's mind.

Let's move on to the point in the story when B arrives. Since G has been waiting for B, it would be good to compose the shot by putting X behind G's shoulder looking past her in the extreme distance as B arrives waving to G : Hello, I'm here, my dear, a little delayed by the heavy traffic,... Next shot? Cut from extreme long to a medium close on B. In this transition, X has jumped twenty feet without any jerk because X has performed an action on behalf of G. She would like to get closer to B, but she cannot jump twenty feet. X can. Please jump on her behalf. Here X has performed an action on behalf of G, a character in the story.

Some time later, B and G argue about something. Since a scene of argument will have the feeling of conflict, it is best to separate them in alternating medium shots and close-ups while they talk. The order of shots will be : G says to X , B replies to X, G talks to X , B talks to X, and so on, and when the shots will be joined it will seem that G has talked to B. Here X acts as a medium through which B and G communicate with each other.

All this is, of course elementary film making technique. **The point of this exercise** is to explain that a film is made by keeping the camera-mike at a position where the the action between the characters can be seen-heard best. Think of **a psychological centre** created by the interaction between the characters. The camera-mike is always placed at this psychological centre, which, of course will keep on shifting as the relation between the characters goes on changing. **In effect, the camera-mike is placed in accordance of the expressive intent of the artist. The movement of the psychological centre creates a contour of relevance in terms of the vision of the artist**. The contour of relevance gives a clue to the choices made by the artist. In the simple example of the B and G story, the camera-mike is shifted over the shots in such a manner as to express the quality of waiting and of meeting and of parting. The camera-mike builds a contour in accordance with the demands of the story of the film.

Incidentally, here we can identify **the source of fan worship of film actors**. The love scene between the Hero and Heroine had actually taken place between the Hero and Heroine and X, the camera-mike, that is, the Spectator, who is in the most advantageous position in the enterprise. We can also see how film puts the spectator in the most advantangeous position for enjoyment of **the pleasure packet of a popular film** where real problems of life are solved by dream solutions.

Whole-Part Relationship in Film Image

A film as a Whole is made up of several Parts. The relationship of a whole to its parts is basic to perception and to the understanding of any film. The film maker arranges the parts in one specific manner because **this arrangement causes the emergence of the function (the meaning) of the whole**. In other words, it is only this arrangement of parts which expresses the structure and shape of feeling of the whole. A Part contributes to making of the Whole, and in turn, derives its own meaning from the Whole.

Take a rough and ready example of a modest element like an umbrella in two scenes. In PP 33, as the raindrop falls on a bald man's head, he opens the umbrella using it for its primary function of protection from rain.

In another scene (PP 36) some day after the stormy night when Durga had died,

Apu comes down from the verandah for going out with a bottle of oil, he halts in the courtyard, looks up at the sky, goes back in the room and we wait till he comes out with an umbrella under his arm. Here, the whole action determines the meaning of the umbrella as a sign of Apu's growing maturity.

Structure and Function of Film Image

Artists make images. An image will be shaped out of some material. This material may be picked up from the real world of life as it is lived, or it can also be based on assumptions, say a lion, as in a fable an animal can speak. For making the structure of the art work, the artist chooses the elements of the structure and the relationships between the elements. The structure that is created then functions to generate meanings and perceptions of themes for the receiver of the work of Art.

The situation can be understood **as an interplay between two worlds**. One is **the world of reality** with its order and chaos, and with its natural and human laws, and with its history. The other is **the world of fiction**, of the images created by the artist. The artist has a vision of some aspect of life, and he expresses it in the image by using materials from the real world and put them in relationships that create a **contour of relevance** which is valid for the original vision.The image as perceived by the receiver emerges from how the artist organises the material in the process of creation.

The world of images is possible because **human understanding works in two ways**. One is the **direct way of perceiving and making sense**. The other is the way of **understanding metaphorically**.

The typical example would be how I understand an expression in ordinary conversation like a friend telling me: 'You are a patch of green in my arid life'. I understand the quality of feeling implied in the sentence. When 'arid' and 'green' are put together the heightened contrast brings out the value of the relationship of my friend with me, and also with the rest of my friend's life. My friend has said nothing about the 'arid' treatment received in real life. Yet, by creating the image my friend succeeds in putting across the meaning-feeling duo in a single sentence, understood by not taking the terms 'arid' and 'patch of green' literally. **They are metaphoric, that is, the words say one thing but mean another. The capacity of human beings to make metaphors and to receive them makes the world of fiction possible.**

The images are structured by using the ordinary dimensions of characteristics of material and arranging them in a manner so that they are invested with meaning-feeling. Let us take a simple example. It is common experience to come across the image of a large figure of the sitting Buddha in meditation in the centre and several small-sized disciples around in postures of surrender or prayer. We understand this arrangement immediately. The small-big visual dimension is being used to express the small-big spiritual attainment.

Artists try to discover ways in which they can say one thing and mean another. They try **to discover the rules of equivalence in terms of feeling in order to create images.** The rules are not fixed. They are constantly being discovered and absorbed in the system of language.

The need for expression in chidren is so strong that they are forced to use whatever language they have, as can be seen in their words, drawings or actions. A child drew a tusker with white blotches in the big belly. Asked to explain why, the child explained that's where the tusks come from. Driving along a road with a lot of potholes, a child remarked that this road should be called Khadbad road. A child makes the drawing of a railway line with a train halted on the station. When asked: Where is the opposite platform? The child halts for a moment and then he goes ahead to write the name of the station in a mirror image on the other side of the line. These examples indicate the source from which metaphoric understanding builds up. The artists contribute to the language (in whichever medium) by creating expressive structures that say one thing and mean another in a complex way.

The structure of the whole film can be grasped by identifying its parts. The parts are bound by the relationships within the whole. **The structure can be identified at three levels. The first level** consists of the foundation of a web of themes expressed by the artist. **The second level** is the narrative structure consisting of scenes and sequences. This level is the **macrostructure** level. **The third level** is visual shots, the sound shots and the editing devices. This is the **microstructure** level.These three levels of structure in a film are interdependent.

Structures are functional. This seems to be a principle of structures in Nature. This principle is copied and used by human beings when they make artificial structures for meeting the needs of some functions of living. Consider some ready examples of structures in Nature. The **skeleton structure of a human being** is different from the **skeleton structure of a fish** since the human beings and the fish function in different environments.

Structures decide the limits and possibilities of the functions of the organisms. When human beings make articles of use, like the handle of a stick or a house, they craft the materials to serve the specific functions of the stick or the house. However, when a human being makes an image, the act of composition is guided by the need for artistic expression. This will be discussed by and by.

Let us pick up the example of the making of a house. If an architect was asked to make a house for me, he would pose the question 'What do I need the house for?' I would say: 'How silly! Of course, I need to live in it.' He will then ask me to detail what I mean by "living". And then I will find myself describing a complex set of functions involving me and my family in a diverse range of activities. The architect will think at my level of current income, decide on a space and then make the division of this chosen space in terms of a drawing room, bedrooms, kitchen, and space for my children and for my parents who live with me, and so on. He will design a house that gives privacy to the members of my family and space for interactions with visitors. The design of my house in this case would be very different from the design of a house for a newly married couple or professionals who spend most of the day at their office and come home only for a limited period of time.

If we look at the structure-function relationship in these examples, we will sense that the design of my house is expressive of an aspect of my living. **When artists compose images, the structure of an image is expressive of the complex vision of feelings and meanings.** In order to understand any film, it is necessary to unravel the design emerging out of the expressive structure.

We can look at our own experience to understand what we mean by the **complexity of design of images**. Take a rough and ready example. I am from a small town, and I have come to a big city college, and I keep telling everyone that Principal Dr. Rao is a good man. Reconstruct the experience which makes me think that Rao is a good man. I had a letter of introduction from my headmaster who knows Rao. However, I was very diffident and tense when I went to Rao's bungalow. As I rang the bell, there was loud music inside the house. The door was opened by a young boy. He turned down the volume of the music and smiled at me. In the meanwhile Mrs. Rao came out, asked me to come in from the uncomfortable verandah and sit in the cool drawing room, adjusted the fan , and asked why I wanted to meet the Principal. She took the letter from me. By this time Dr. Rao also came out. When he knew my background, he accepted me with hearty friendliness. Mrs. Rao went in, and after a while brought cups of coffee for us. The Principal assured me of all the help.

In this total happening, the 'goodness' of Dr. Rao is made up of several elements occurring together, the assurance of help by Rao, the feeling of welcome by the family, the small courtesies, the polite behaviour of the son and Mrs. Rao, even the daintiness of the cups in which coffee, brought for me as if I were a special guest. The daintiness of coffee cups is related to the 'goodness' of Dr. Rao as **an overtone**.

The concept of overtone comes from acoustics. When you pluck a string or a tuning fork, it generates the note N , and also notes of fractions of the original note, N/2, N/4, N/8..., which are called overtones. **The richness of sound of main tone N is due to the presence of overtones of N.** When artists create images, they enrich the main theme by also bringing within the composition the overtones of the main theme. If a film tells the story of a poor family, the main theme may be in terms of the low earnings of the breadwinner, but the quality of the house, clothes, pots and pans, will come into the composition of shots as overtones to support the main theme in numerous ways.

Design in Film

While analyzing a work like the Apu Trilogy, our best guide is **the Design**.The design emerges from the expressive whole created through the arrangement of the material. The whole needs to be interpreted in its own parts. The whole-part relationships in the film have to be understood as an order of sequences and of scenes in the **macrostructure.** The devices of **microstructure** have to be identified in order to understand the logic of what the filmmaker wishes to express.The thematic web has to be unraveled to catch the nuances of expression.

The next chapter is all about Design and how it can be identified in the Apu Trilogy.

Chapter 2

DESIGN IN THE APU TRILOGY

The Apu Trilogy offers two alternatives for a critical study. Treat each film as an independent unit or treat the three films together as one whole. Each film PATHER PANCHALI (PP), APARAJITO (APJT) and APUR SANSAR (AS) shows Apu's growth during well defined periods of his life. The Trilogy itself has a kind of similarity between the way it begins and ends. The beginning has events six years after Apu's birth, when important things happen around him when he is too young to influence them. However, these events certainly contribute to his growth. At the end of the Trilogy, Apu is now a father when he begins the first personal contact with his son Kajal, six years after his birth.

Macrostructure

Now we begin the first probe into the macrostructure with the primary objective of **identifying elements of the design**. Notice the obvious rhythm that the Trilogy has three films and **each film has a three Part division**. This division follows the internal logic of the plot within a film. For PP and APJT, **the first part** sets up a life style by the interaction of the characters in the foreground environment. **The second part** shows the stresses in the pattern, which also increase in intensity. In **the third part**, the main event is the snapping of some bond which held the pattern together. This snap will move the action away from this location to somewhere else. AS also has a three part structure, but it varies in the content of parts and in the manner they connect to make the whole film. In AS the making of the pattern is followed by the shattering of the pattern and ultimately results in the beginning of a new relationship.

Nischindipur, Manasaopta, and Aparna's nameless village in the Khulna area are fictional locations in east Bengal, now Bangladesh. The city of Benares on the river Ganga in east Uttar Pradesh, has several names. Kashi is holy name for the pilgrims. Varanasi is the sanskritised version and now the official name. The secular variant, Benares, is extensively used in the period of the story and even now.

We use Benares which is closer to the overall feeling of the fiction played out in the city. Similarly, Calcutta is now spelt Kolkata. However, the time period of the film suggests that we use the original spelling Calcutta when referring to the city.

PATHER PANCHALI

Part 1: Apu's father, Harihar Ray struggles to live with his family in the ancestral village, Nishchindipur. Six years pass after Apu's birth. At one point he leaves the village temporarily to make money earnings elsewhere.

Part 2 : While Harihar is away, difficulties continue to increase for Apu's mother, Sarbojaya, climaxing on the night of the house collapse and death of Durga, Apu's sister.

Part 3 : Harihar abandons the ancestral house and migrates with his family to Benares.

APARAJITO

Part 1 : The new pattern of life in Benares collapses with Harihar's sudden death. Sarbojaya's effort to hold on cannot provide for Apu's proper growth. She returns to live in the village Manasapota in Bengal with support from an uncle.

Part 2 : At Manasapota, Apu starts work as a priest and also goes to school. Six years pass. Apu wins a scholarship after matriculation but has to overcome Sarbojaya's reluctance to permit him to go to Calcutta for college studies.

Part 3 : With Apu away in Calcutta, Sarbojaya is left alone in the village, withering away steadily, eventually sinking to her death. With snapping of the last family bond, Apu takes the final decision to abandon the ancestral profession of priesthood and seek alternative possibilities opened up by further studies in Calcutta.

APUR SANSAR

Part 1 : In Calcutta Apu is isolated, when Pulu pulls him out and takes him along to Khulna. In a sudden turn of chance events, Apu gets married to Aparna and the two decide to live a life based on trust and transparency.

Part 2: In Calcutta Apu and Aparna set up a world of togetherness in happy marriage. This is shattered by Aparna's death in childbirth. Apu in depression isolates himself from the social life around and from his own creative work.

Part 3 : Six years pass in Khulna as Apu's son, Kajal, grows up devoid of any parental contact while Apu moves far and wide aimlessly. Pulu pulls Apu out of isolation again. Apu comes to see Kajal, tries and succeeds in finding a method of bonding with the child.

PP can be divided into three Parts

at the two points when Harihar goes away from the village, first temporarily for more earning, and the second time with finality when he has decided to abandon the ancestral house and migrate to Benares.

Likewise, the two points which divide APJT in three parts are also the points of moving away: first, when Sarbojaya leaves Benares for Manasapota, and the second when Apu forces his decision for going to Calcutta for higher education.

The design of AS varies from the other two films in the manner it begins and ends. It begins with Apu in isolation and ends on Apu making a bond with his son. Establishing a new bond is the very opposite of the bond-snapping endings of PP and of APJT, which prompt the question: What next for Apu? In contrast, the AS ending affirms life values in a novel manner when the estranged father Apu and son Kajal meet and Apu accepts the next generation Kajal as a friend, not merely as a son.

Let us have an overview of the total design of the Trilogy. **When the three films are placed together they generate a spiral shape**. PP has the inner structure with the following rhythm. At first, the setting up of a pattern of bonds – then, the bond is seen under stress – last, the bonds snap. Harihar's family which is rooted in the ancestral village is under stress and eventually has to abandon their ancestral place and move to Benares in search of the higher level of a more dignified living. In APJT, the movements are – Benares, to the village Manasapota, and finally Apu's movement away from the village to Calcutta, as also from the profession that tradition had offered him. The movement for holding on to a pattern and away from it gets to another higher level at the end of APJT. AS begins with Apu's search for dignity in isolation. He goes through an intense period of togetherness which is also shattered. Eventually a new pattern of dignity in Apu's acceptance of his son takes the end of the Trilogy to the highest level of the spiral like movement of the three films. **The textual analysis of films will reveal in detail how this spiral shape is formed** as Apu's story unfolds on the screen.

The **devices of creating meaningful wholes** are identified as the filmmaker's expression in the cinematic language. The visual and sound components and their relationships reveal a design that tells us the story as well as the comment and suggestion of the filmmaker. The ways of identifying the elements and units and the ways of stating the relationships are detailed here.

Here we start the exploration by asking **two questions**: What are the organising principles of the narrative structure of Trilogy? What are the audio-visual devices which reveal the narrative in the film medium? It is often a difficult first exercise to break down a well integrated film into its analytical segments. Hence, an exploratory question: **What is this film about?** could initiate the process of understanding how the film has been put together as a whole.

We can supplement this by another exercise. Select a detail from the film and ask the question: **What is this detail doing here?** This will lead us to discover the several ways in which the selected detail gets linked up with details in other parts of the film. Every detail is part of a meaningful whole. The relationships of such meaningful wholes create the total film. Through such explorations of whole-part relationships, it is possible to identify three levels of structure in a film.

One, a thematic structure like a web of strands of various kinds.

Two, a macrostructure that holds together the design of the narrative.

Three, a microstructure created by the choice of visual, sound and editing details which function to reveal the story and also express the themes in the cinematic language.

Here we attempt to explain the manner in which the three levels are integrated in the Trilogy. The first exploratory question: **What is this film about?** also helps us understand the very purpose of creation of the film and its relevance as a work of art.

What is the Trilogy about? The answer is that the Trilogy is about a web of themes. This web can be traced by working along the following lines. The foreground fictional characters operate in the background of the Indian reality of a specific time period, 1910 to about 1935. This reality has two aspects:

One, the immediate physical and social environment of the period

Two, the remote complex of systems which controls the administrative power and the economy of that time period.

The immediate environment has a system of socio-religious settings, like the family and the community, operating with traditional norms. The remote systems influence the immediate, causing some foreground fictional characters to move from the rural context to the urban. These changes, both in the foreground and background, influence the life of feeling of the characters in the Trilogy.

The thematic web of the Trilogy is made by the lines of influence which crisscross mainly in three areas of change. Forces of economic change are pushing away the unwilling village people towards the city in search of survival. The fast weakening village system is under such severe pressures that survival with dignity for traditional people is getting increasingly difficult. The traditional economy is changing to the money economy so that cash in hand matters more in day-to-day living. The third area is Education. The British introduced the educational system as a multilayered device for maintaining administrative control on the Indian people. Education brought with it a world of knowledge, as also a social view in daily living which was new for Indians. The new education also prepared Indians for steady, graded jobs with fixed cash pay, unlike anything in the traditional Indian economy. The social reality with Brahmins at the top changed as the traditional means of survival became inadequate and forced them towards the city that had larger options for earning a living.

Analytical Tool - Motifs

For the study of a complex work like the Trilogy, we need versatile tools capable of probing the structure at various levels. Our **essential tools are two kinds of enquiry**. **One**: identify **the motifs** which interact to generate the force of progression in the narrative. A motif, by its very nature, is repetitive. If we look for recurrent units in the narrative which repeat or appear with variation, we can get to the motifs and their manner of interplay. **Two**: the other tool of enquiry traces **the binding principles** which connect diverse elements and make the film a rhythmic entity. **The four main binding principles are similarity and contrast, balance and resolution**. Similarity and contrast are complementary, so also balance and resolution. If we observe how the principles of similarity and contrast or balance and resolution operate in connecting diverse elements in the film, it could provide useful understanding of what the film is saying directly or metaphorically.

We will first talk of motifs and later of binding principles.

The motif as a unit of design can be drawn from any level of the film. **A direct audio-visual image** on the screen can be a motif if it recurs. Recall the visual composition of mirror shots in PP where Durga applies bindi and kajal, Apu tries to hold a paper moustache and in AS when Aparna applies *sindur* and *bindi*. At another level, a character like a friendly neighbour can be a motif and so also a relationship between characters like husband and wife.

A motif can also be **a shape which is not seen physically but sensed** in the interaction of characters. Think of **the triangles of tension** in the guava stealing episode at the beginning of PP. A motif has **variations** and **overtones**. Recall the railways in various aspects as they appear in all the three films, like the trains, the platform, the engine, the tracks, the passengers in the interior of a railway compartment, and so on.

Motifs at the same level can be **linked in a sequential order**. For example, take the act of pilfering. Durga pilfers fruit now, she continues to pilfer six years later. Indir pilfers, so also Ranu, each in her own circumstances, even Sarbojaya pilfers.

Linking can also join motifs at different **vertical levels**, the verticality itself may be in the structure or be conceptual. Think of a vertically connected linkage like Apu's books, which appears in all the three films but gets invested with different meanings with Apu's intellectual growth. Books are conceptually related to Apu's education, which in turn is related to the larger process of schools and colleges as a method of change in society.

Linkages of this kind cause **density of details** which, in turn, enhances the richness of meaning. Think of the sources of light. The oil lamp that Sarbojaya carries in PP and the lantern that appears beneath the departing bullock cart and is carried through APJT and to Apu's first experience of switching on and off the wonder of electric light. And in AS, switching on with a vengeance. And of course, the sun lighting up in infinite shades, the first sun rays on the Benares ghats, the slowly fading Nischindipur evenings. Lighting is a matter of the environment and of the technology level of the location on the screen.

Let us now look for **motifs which help generate the narrative design** of the Trilogy. The main motif in the foreground fiction is Apu's family since the narration moves along portraying what happens to Apu's family. It begins with Apu's birth, and goes through distinct stages of childhood, adolescence and youth. It ends almost twenty five years later when Apu connects with the next generation, his son, Kajal.

Apu's family would include, besides Apu himself, relatives like father, mother, sister and a distant aunt like Indir, and later, a wife and son.

These persons would generate numerous interrelations. Any of these, for example mother-daughter relationship, could be used as a new motif in the design. This understanding of the fictional family is firmly based in the Indian reality where the family network provides a secure identity to the individual from sources like parental surname and lineage.

A neighbour's family is like a variation of the main motif and it enters the design to the extent it is relevant to the main family. For example, Shejobou's family has no male member entering the plot, since it is not relevant. When someone from Apu's family links with someone in the neighbour's family, like Durga and Ranu, it sets up a new motif.

Apu has playmates in PP and APJT, one of them, Shambhu is teaching him English. At the college in Calcutta he shares the time out of the class with Shibnath in the early days. Later, in AS he finds a bond of friendship with Pulu who pulls Apu out of his loneliness and isolation. Apu differs in this respect from Harihar. Harihar's social circle is limited by his priestly profession.

The abstract term 'living' has physical counterparts, like houses to dwell in, food to eat, clothes to wear and for decoration, as also other essentials for living like water and light. All these would also enter the design in numerous varied details. A component from the house like a door can also be a significant motif used in different contexts to portray different events in the life of the characters. A family faces numerous issues, like prestige, income, expenses, education, health, and more. One could be talking about any of them or working on some aspect of it.....and each of these could become a motif.

Events in the narration occur against the backdrop of natural and social environment. Many elements in the environment recur in a cyclical manner. A cycle can be man made like the repetitive routine of work every morning, or it could originate from Nature like day and night, or the change of season, and of birth and death. **A cycle is also repetitive but it is not the same as motif**. When a motif repeats, the narrative is carried forward. As the narrative moves forward it can meet the cycle at several points. This sets up the possibility of comparing or contrasting two elements which are otherwise distant from each other. Such connections between remote elements provide rhythm to the body of the work as a whole. Sometimes these connections can set up metaphors. Hence the cycle is best considered as a binding principle and distinguished from a motif. We will think about binding principles a little later.

In the design of narration, characters seen as **individuals, pairs or trios** can be considered motifs. The way they are shaped, their similarities and contrasts make the design of characters over the whole film. Apu and his immediate family are in the foreground fiction. What happens to them makes the main story. They interact with other characters which appear as parts of the community, or outsiders coming to the village for different occasions. The texture of the community is created by their specific images contributing their bit to the density of portrayal.

The environment inevitably appears in any visual frame. The Trilogy contains a design of the environment in which Apu's life gets shaped. There are two aspects of the environment, the natural and the man-made. Details of both types are included in the design. They create the texture of the cycles of seasons and the community events. In case of the manmade systems, they too appear in the visual detail and in the actions of characters. For instance, the postal service is referred to by numerous letters being written or received, and in PP we see the tail end of the postal system when Apu comes in running with the postcard and drops it like a postman. The railways and the educational system are portrayed in a more direct manner on the screen.

It is also possible to think of **the shapes of scenes in graphic terms**. A point is created by a single character. A line is created by two persons, whereas a triangle can be created by three persons. There could be variations created by the changing shapes of the interactions. The triangular shape may be perceived in the interactions. Similarly, a circular shape may be created by the dynamics of a scene. The arrangement of the triangular and the circular scenes is an aspect of the macro structure. Within the dynamics of the design, a complex motif may develop and, in the process, create other lines and shapes.

Analytical Tool - Binding Principles

The other essential tool is the identification of binding principles which hold the work together as a rhythmic entity. When a motif repeats, it causes progression of narration. A binding principle also repeats, but its primary function is to establish connections between narrative elements which are far apart. These connections help in holding the body of the work as a rhythmic whole. Some such connections may also **create metaphors which help to comprehend some nuances of the life of feeling,** an area of experience which is otherwise inarticulable. **The most common binding principles are similarity and contrast, balance and resolution**. It is convenient to put together similarity and contrast since they are complementary, and so also balance and resolution.

Similarity and Contrast

When the narration suggests a routine, it is achieved through use of **repetitive details**. For example, in the morning routine for a household a detail like getting water for the day can repeat in the narration. In PP, water is fetched in pots from the well in Shejobou's compound. In APJT, the tap supplies water to the courtyard right inside the house in Benares, but the holy water is to be brought from the river Ganga. The Manasapota village house has a well of its own. The Calcutta building in AS has a ground floor tap connection all right, but the women there are heard complaining that it is dried up this morning when it is needed most. Ironically, it is raining heavily and the rainwater gutter is pouring down a heavy stream of water.

Likewise, think of **relations with neighbours as an element which provides a similarity-contrast binding across the Trilogy**. PP sets up the contrast of Shejobou and Nilmoni's Wife. The Benares house in APJT has a good neighbour like Pandey coexisting with the sly Nandababu. The AS terrace level room has a wide range of neighbours, notably Pintu's mother who tries to coax some food into the grieving Apu, and the anonymous girl waiting on the opposite window, as also the ground floor namesake A.K.Roy who can mess up letters meant for Apu. Such minor elements abound in the Trilogy. Let us now pick up a large complex unit like marriage, and see how similarity and contrast work through it as a binding principle in the body of narration in the Trilogy.

There are **two marriage events** in the Trilogy, of Ranu and of Apu. They are similar as both are performed with traditional rituals, but they are widely contrasted as they expresss two different aspects of the institution of marriage itself.

Ranu's marriage is an event of public interest and community participation. Ranu, the person directly concerned has decided to accept all decisions of the family elders from the very beginning when the proposal was private knowledge shared only with intimate friends. The information becomes public when the date of the marriage is fixed. The actual celebrations of the marriage are presented on public externals like excitement around the playing band and active presence of neighbours in front of the bride's house. Moving inside, the opulence continues on large quantities of food for feasting cooked by the women of the community. We move in further to the bride's room but here too we see the externals like the decoration of the bride. The final hand-holding ritual does not even identify the bridegroom as a person. It is Ranu's hand in the hand of a man who has the approval of Ranu'elders.

Apu's marriage is composed in a sharply different manner. It passes through some very rapid development. There is a crisis. Aparna's proposed bridegroom is discovered to be insane and is rejected. According to belief, the girl will be cursed if the auspicious hour of ten in the night is missed. So a bridegroom has to be found. The elders and Pulu approach Apu, who at first rejects the very idea. However, sensing the acute disgrace faced by the bride's family, Apu persuades himself to think that he is doing a noble act by agreeing to marry Aparna, even though he has nothing to support it back in Calcutta, no proper living space, no resources, not even a regular salaried job. Pulu promises him one. Apu does not have even a clean shirt to wear for the marriage ceremony. Pulu gives him one. However, after the wedding Apu gives absolute priority to begin building up a relationship with Aparna based on trust and transparency by ensuring that all the material facts about him are known to her, and more importantly, she is confident of going with him immediately to Calcutta and share his poor life. Apu treats marriage as a personal matter of mutual trust between man and wife.

We also notice the design of macrostructure how the opulence of Ranu's marriage is contrasted by placing it between two scenes of severe depletion in Sarbojaya's household. (end of PP 28 and beginning of PP 30). Also this contrast is further intensified within the wedding sequence itself (PP 29). The sequence is done in three parts, and in each part one member of the poor family is centrally placed with respect to display of opulence. Apu is shown centrally with respect to the band players in the outer area of the bride's house. In the middle area, Sarbojya is physically handling the plenitude of food for feasting. In the interior, Durga's smile has a pensive strain as she enjoys watching the elaborate bridal makeup and the wedding rituals.

The births and deaths in the Trilogy form a well organized design of their own. The two births are sharply contrasted. Apu's birth, the birth of a son is truly a happy event for the family and the community. When Apu's son is born, the mother dies; happiness is neutralised by its tragic contrast. The fiction of the Trilogy places deaths as ruthless turning points. Indir is very old, in any case due to die soon but she asserts her dignity in the manner she dies. Durga has just entered youth when she dies of a mere fever in a poor medical help situation. Harihar's death is all too sudden, when he was settling down to a new pattern of living in Benares. With Apu distancing, Sarbojaya slowly withers away in silent loneliness in the village. Aparna's death while giving life to Kajal fits well in the design of life-death in the Trilogy.

Balance and Resolution

The binding principle of balance and resolution regulates the structure of narration as follows. **When a motif develops under its own logic to a point of imbalance, a fresh balancing element has to be brought in for the resolution of tension caused by the imbalance**. Pick up an example. Think of Apu-Sarbojaya distancing as a motif, which increases over the years. Apu's education in modern subjects has opened up his awareness of the wide world and of alternative methods of living, which shifts him away from any compulsions of his priestly origin. Over these years, even though Sarbojaya's sole focus is on Apu, she continues cherishing traditional ideas around the family profession of priesthood. After sometime, Apu even avoids going to the village for a two day holiday, and sends her money as if in compensation. She would not let Apu be informed of her illness, as if making the point that Apu should come on his own, and not because he is called. The distancing has stretched to a breaking point. The resolution of the imbalance is Sarbojaya's death. It comes as if with the evening train which makes Sarbojaya hallucinate that Apu has come to her. She drags herself to the poolside as distant animals howl and the fireflies dance in the gathering darkness and, very simply, she dies there. The death also snaps Apu's last bond with the family and confirms his decision to abandon the family profession and seek alternatives opened up by his education.

Think of one more example of balance and resolution as a binding principle. For six years Apu had kept on rejecting his son under the insistent self-belief that Kajal's birth was responsible for Aparna's death. After interaction with Pulu, Apu goes and meets Kajal. The innocence and vulnerability of the child makes Apu recognize the significance of Kajal as the continuation of Aparna's love. This new realisation resolves his long standing tension and he accepts the responsibility for the son.

Microstructure

The analysis of Microstructure in a film design involves **two kinds of observations. One**, the visual details and simultaneous sound details which are seen-heard on the screen, and **two**, the order in which the shots are placed to make the scene. The spectator experiences the narration by receiving from the screen these two simultaneously. Hence identifying these two processes is important for understanding the working of the film medium. The director's choice of audio-visual details creates a microstructure that is integral to the expression of themes. This integration can be unravelled. For this purpose we can identify the links of meaning at the narrative level, as also at the thematic level. Remember Indir and recall her face, clothes, gait and walk, her stick and pot, her rags and mat and her story telling voice and her song. All of these express the old character, her poverty and her rootedness. Her gestures and actions bring out the value issues as well. The microstructure in the Trilogy carefully portrays and expresses the characters and the themes as we will see in the next chapter. The principles of microstructure are outlined here.

Seeing is different from hearing. The expressive characteristics of any visual element are based on space while for the audio they are based on time and on tone. Hence, the micro-level study of visuals and of sound need different analytical terms. The expressive quality of the finished film is based on the picture-sound combination in simultaneity and also in succession.

The expressive power of the visual depends on its graphic foundation. Lines, drawn or created, express certain feelings by their very graphic characteristics. All human beings on Earth are subject to the vertical pull of gravity, and this affects the way in whch one responds to lines. A vertical line feels strong and also stable because it is defying gravity. A horizontal line feels restful and also stable because it is not defying gravity. A diagonal line is tense because it is subjected to two opposite pulls of stability, the horizontal from one side and the vertical from the other. A curve will be more suggestive of options of twists and turns and suggest what a straight line would not be able to communicate.

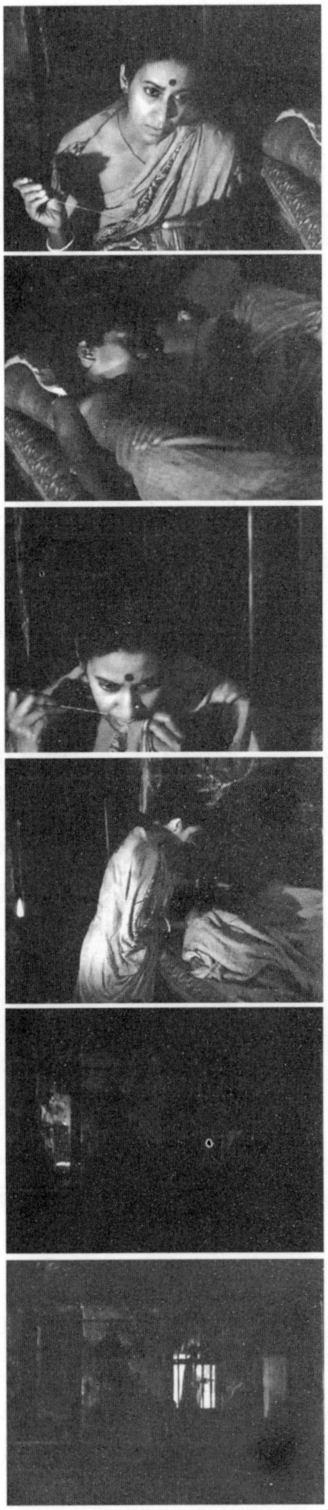

In the Trilogy, the relationship can be seen to be explicit in directing spectator response along a contour of relevance. If we look at the sequence of scenes and their shapes of feeling, the contour of relevance becomes quite explicit. For example, remember the night scene when Sarbojaya decides to sell the costly brass utensils. The light, the pace, the texture of her clothes and the wicker box, the polished surface of the plate with the inscription Besh Thak (Be Happy) followed by the early morning scene when she goes out of the house secretively, ensuring that nobody sees her,with the utensils covered carefully and returns with food grain. The PP Theme music plays in the background. The pressure and the heaviness of her gait, the pathos of the situation come across through the expressive visuals. Here she is trying to cover her predicament, yet the door she closed can hold on no more.

The auditory image exists in time and therefore

has a flowing character. It occurs simultaneously with the moving visual images and creates a more complex unit of the film composition. Sounds have several characteristics that are expressive of different feelings. Sounds from the environment abound. The croaking of frogs on the night of Apu's birth is an example of environmental sound. The sound of human speech brings with it all the complexity of meaning of language and nuances of speech, what is being said by the characters and how. Human speech adds to the meaning of what is being seen. Sarbojaya is called by everyone as notunbou (new sister-in-law). Nilmoni's daughter Bini coins the term notunkhuri (new aunty) for addressing Sarbojaya. This is an example of creation of a new term in the conventional code of address of different persons in the community. Background music highlights meaning of visuals in specific ways. The background music contributes to the texture of film experience.

Analysis at the microstructure level includes the graphic devices, the sound devices and the editing patterns that create the total meaning of the film. Let us see this in some detail in the kitchen scene (PP-7-8-9).

1

2

3

4

5

6

7

8

9

10

14

11

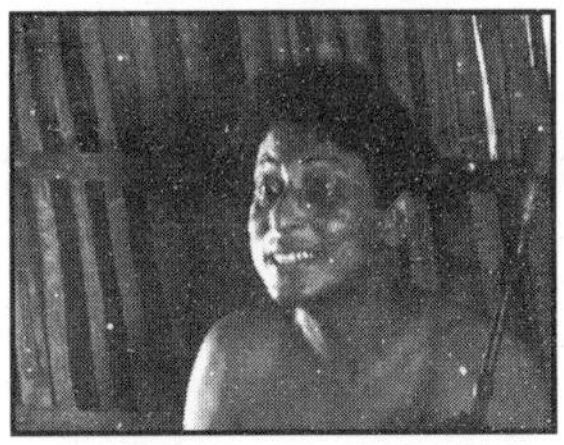

15

12

16

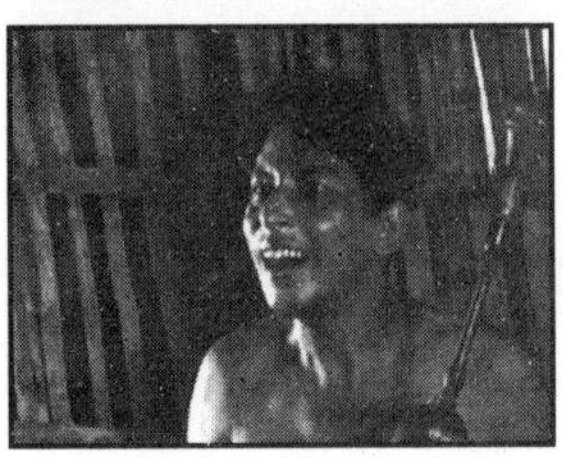

13

17A

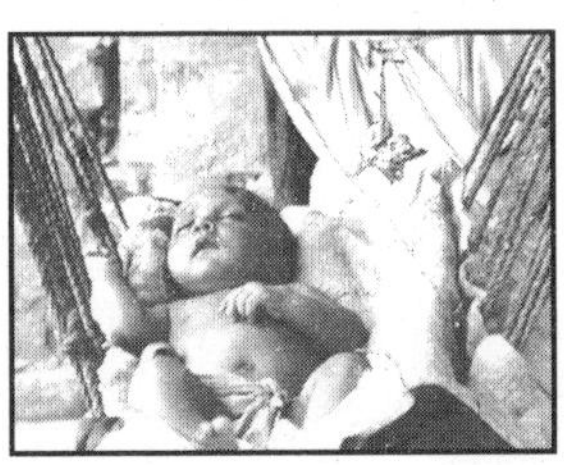

17B

Let us first look at the arrangement of the seventeen shots within the scene. Shot 1 and Shot 2 have Indir with Apu-in-cradle and Durga with toy box on the main verandah.

The next three shots 3, 4 and 5 are in the kitchen hut as Sarbojaya sits cooking and Harihar comes in to sit and talk while smoking his hookah. Shot No. 6 is composed from within the kitchen hut with Sarbojaya and Harihar in the foreground and with the main verandah in the distant back where Indir, Apu-in-cradle and Durga can be seen. The whole family is within the same frame, which **suggests the togetherness of the family.**

The next nine shots (No.7 to 15) are medium or close shots **alternating on Sarbojaya and Harihar emphasizing their seperation.**

Shot No.16 again gets back to **the togetherness of the family** with the same visual composition as of shot no 6, with the difference that Durga now comes in the kitchen hut and sits close to Harihar. Shot No. 17 gets back to Indir and Apu-in-cradle.

The scene follows **a circular shape**. It begins with the very old and very young together, then it moves along as the adults display differences and resolve them, and **it ends the way it had begun**, on the very old and the very young.

1

We now try to get a better understanding of the structure of ths scene. We expand the content of shots with reference to the relevant still.

Shot No. 1: on main verandah opens with a side view tilting down on a relaxed Indir singing a lullaby while swinging the infant Apu in a string cradle. Recall that Indir was not in the house the night Apu was born. She had a tiff with Sarbojaya and had left the house. However, she returned promptly on her own the very next morning and stayed on firmly in the house. She knew she was needed. Five months have now passed. Indir has self-assumed responsibility of looking after the child while Sarbojaya goes about the housework. The lullaby is about a poor person's dream of dressing up the baby as if he is a prince. Six years later one night we will see Indir sit in similar posture singing another song, this time an ardent prayer seeking divine help in making the difficult journey across the river of life.

2

Shot No. 2: on the main verandah is a medium tilting up on Durga counting dried seeds in her toy box. The toy box was first seen when Durga was fast asleep on the night of Apu's

3

4

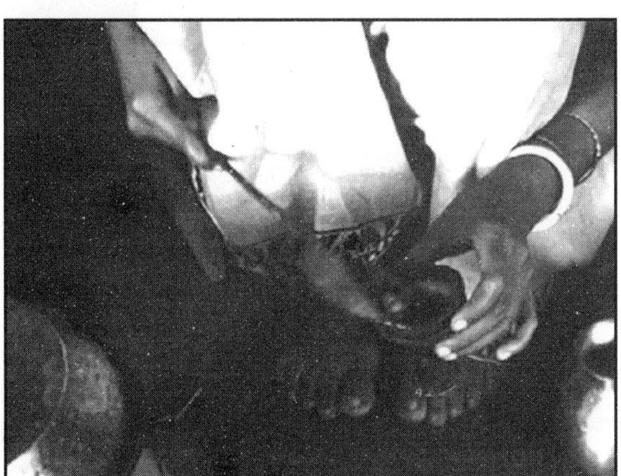

5

birth, and it occurs in several later scenes. When Shejobou comes accusing Durga of necklace theft, the toy box contents are ruthlessly scattered around. After the violent mood has subsided, Indir collects with loving care all the scattered junk back into the box. On the day following the *jatra* performance Durga begins beating up Apu for meddling with her toy box for searching out the junk he had pilfered from her box for making a tinsel crown. Sarbojaya intervenes, trying to shame her that a grown up girl could still be attached to the childish triviality of a toy box.

The next three shots, of very short duration in the kitchen hut, establish and explain Sarbojaya and Harihar in the scene. Sarbojaya is sitting and cooking on the oven, while Harihar comes in asking for cinders for his chillum and sits down to talk while he smokes the hokkah.

Shot No.3: Sarbojaya sitting with oven. Harihar lower half enters frame.

Shot No.4: Kitchen looking at Indir's verandah as Harihar sits down.

Shot No.5: Sarbojaya fills chillum with cinders.

The main verbal exchange

between Harihar and Sarbojaya passes through three stages of feeling: relaxed, then tensed up, then back to relaxed. This three stage feeling structure is also seen in the visual composition and editing of shots.

Shot No. 6: The relaxed segment starts with Harihar talk of a plan of a community feast for celebrating the first-rice ritual of the newly born son, as also the happy prospect of a regular job for him next month onwards. All this is done mainly in a single shot of lengthy duration in which the visual composition includes the entire family. Harihar and Sarbojaya sit in the kitchen foreground with the Indir-Apu combine and Durga in the distant verandah. The quality of shared togetherness is revealed here, as if at source. You see the entire family and at the same time you hear the adults talk of plans of its social prestige and financial stability.

In the second stage of tensing up a doubting Sarbojaya poses a succession of searching questions at Harihar, whose initial response is guarded, even defensive, but he manages to shift fast enough to optimistic articulation. The tension of non-togetherness is caused here by separating Sarbojaya and Harihar in nine shots with such emphasis in visual and editing composition that a shot when including

6

7

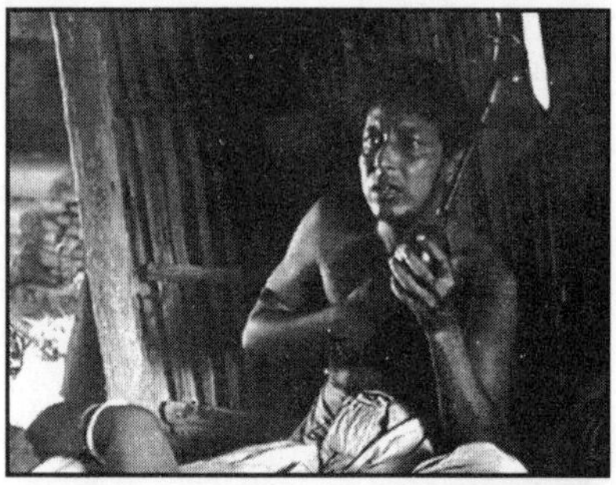

8

9

10

11

12

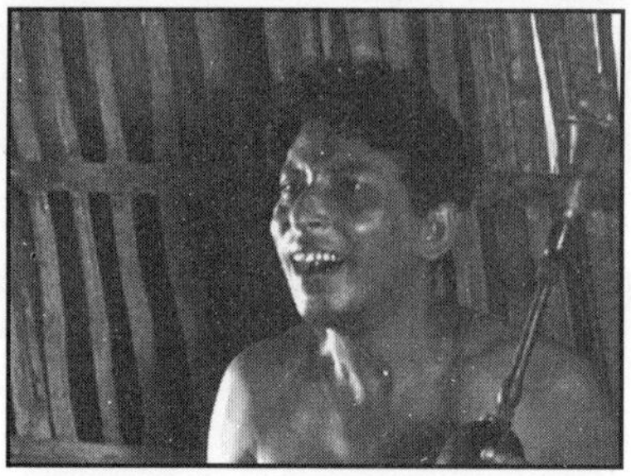

13

14

one person seems to be consciously excluding the other. These nine shots, medium or close, are fixed in alternating order in this segment.

Shot No. 7: You have always been cheated because you are so naive.

Shot No. 8: Why do you say that?

Shot No. 9: Look at the manner in which they cheated you out of our orchard.

Shot No. 10: That was surrendered to repay a loan of three hundred rupees Haran-da had taken from them.

Shot No. 11: We wouldn't have to worry if the orchard was still with us. They take away bagfuls of fruit right from our doorstep, and if Durga picks up even one guava she says such unpleasant things.

Shot No. 12: Harihar : I have nothing to do with them. Let them look after money lending. I will look after my scholarship./ Sarbojaya (offscreen) Who cares for your scholarship in this backward place?./ Harihar: Listen. Let me tell you what I am writing.

Shot No. 13 (Closer on Harihar): I am writing new poetry new plays. Once people know about it, the jatra managers will come flocking to me.

Shot No. 14: Sarbojaya (listening to offscreen Harihar) They want new stuff. That does not grow on trees. The new writers of today are just repeating the old stuff.

15

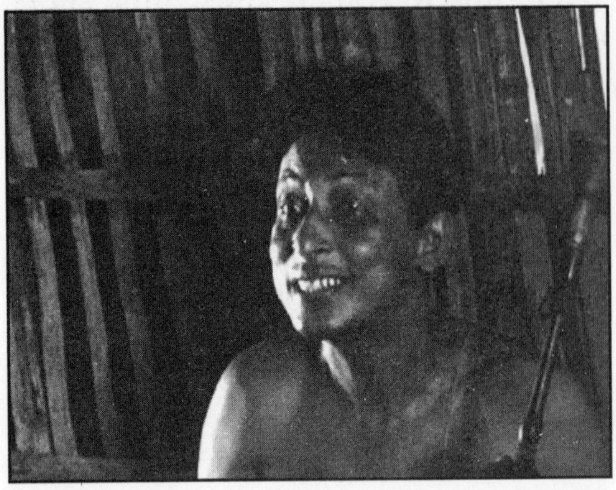

Shot No. 15: Harihar: The same old stuff repeated every time. If that can be accepted why will people not take, pure, original work from Harihar Ray of Nishchindipur.

We move to the third stage as Harihar's optimism works and manages to relax Sarbojaya, changing the feeling tone of the scene to shared togetherness. This quality is achieved in a single shot with more or less the same camera view as the single shot of the first relaxed segment, Shot No. 6.

Shot No. 16: It takes in the entire family. Both adults are in the kitchen and Durga comes in and sits affectionately close to Harihar, while the Indir-Apu combine can also be seen in the distant verandah. The talk is of what Harihar and Sarbojaya are dreaming up for the family in the future. Education and sacred training for Apu, marriage for Durga, two meals a day, change of clothing once a year, paying off of debts, repairs of the house. The PP theme tune comes in the background from the point Durga comes in, and is also continued over the last shot till the end of the scene.

16

In this scene we can see things in the kitchen like pots and pans, a ladle and a bottle on the shelf, also Harihar's hookah which have a used look given to them by constant daily rub. So also the split bamboo door at the back. In

17A

fact, the entire house has a lived-in feeling, which is stimulated when interesting human action occurs against the worn out look of the house. Like Sarbojaya's gesture of reacting to oven heat as she sits cooking contributes to the lived in feeling of the kitchen hut.

Shot No. 17-A: Indir, dosing herself, but steady about Apu in cradle. **Camera tilts down**

Shot No.17-B: Sleeping infant Apu, the son of the family, focus of love of all.

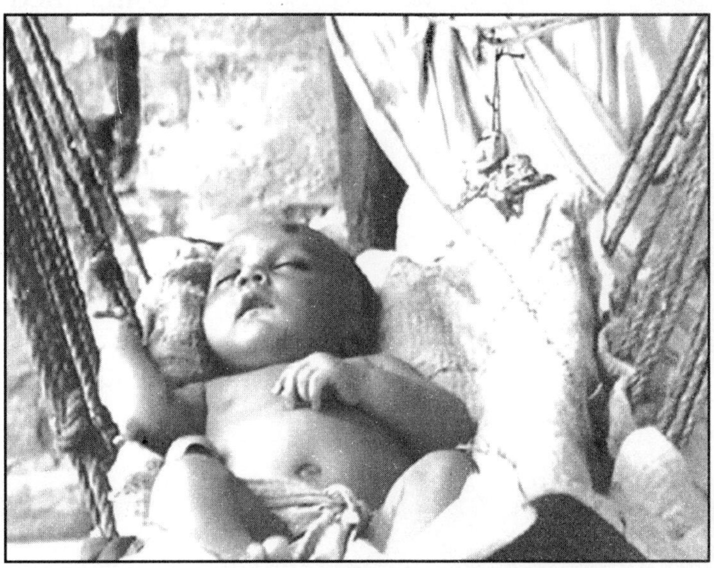

17B

The visual similarity between infant Apu and Apu's infant son is striking as also the contrast of the singing Indir and in Kajal's case, the sighing grandmother. A generation later Apu's son Kajal, deprived of mother and of father, will swing in an ornate cradle, accompanied only by the grandmother's sighs, which matches the sound of the sea waves in the next shot. (AS 56)

Music in Design

Music can operate in design as motif as also binding principle. Music as such, is abstract in the sense that it has no referential meaning. It has the capacity to stimulate feelings in the listener. The foreground visual scene interacts with background music to create an audio-visual combination capable of expressing new ideas. In associating with the visual content, a music piece acquires the new referential association even as it continues to carry the original feeling.

The Trilogy uses background music in several ways for narration. **The title music** of each film has an element of sound of one tune dominant. For our convenience; we are naming the dominant tunes in the films as PP Theme Tune or APJT Tune or AS Theme Tune. In PP and AS the Theme Tune also occurs at the end of the film. A tune from one film can be used in other films to connect events which are far apart in time. These connections could be of several kinds. Let us pick up one tune, say the PP Theme Tune and follow it across the Trilogy.

PP: the film shows how pressures of change force Apu's father Harihar to abandon his ancestral home in the village and shift with family to the city of Benares in search of a dignified life. **The PP Theme Tune** provides a frame to this narrative development, since the film begins with and also ends with it (PP 45). **Within the film it recurs nine times**, underlining the core elements in the family as a rural entity. Early in the film with the five months old Apu in cradle, the Tune rounds off a kitchen scene as Sarbojaya and Harihar outline their modest dreams (PP 8-9). When the film ends the Tune caresses the sad faces of the decimated family, with all dreams shattered they move away from the abandoned village home. (PP 45). During the film the versatile Tune recurs over a range of events, heart warming to heart breaking. The Tune, as if protects Sarbojaya from peering eyes as she moves out of the door with utensils to pawn them and bring back bare survival grain (PP 28). It increases the pleasure of seeing the playing children return home with the calf as evening falls (PP 14), and also on the day they run much far out to hear the telegraph poles and to see the train. (PP 22) Returning from that adventure the Tune accompanies Apu and Durga (PP 23) happily back into the bamboo grove where the beloved Indir sits hunched up, but now beyond any fun, dead. The Tune underlines Durga on the morning she begins learning household jobs like sweeping the courtyard (PP 3). And on Durga again, eyes glazed in high fever, unaware of the passing sweetseller on the quiet evening before of the stormy night she dies (PP 34). It escorts Apu on way to his first day at school (PP 12).

The PP Theme Tune moves into APJT twice, on both occasions referring to Bengal. We hear it on the morning landscape of the countryside as the train from Benares comes into Bengal bringing back on it Sarbojaya and Apu, with the mere trace of smile on her face.(APJT 30) Recall the very last shot of PP where the Theme Tune had seen Sarbojaya hide her sobbing face while leaving for Benares(PP 45). The Tune seems to contain between that sob and this smile the Benares episode for Sarbojaya. Also, not surprisingly we hear it on the Inspector, a dark faced Bengali person dressed in immaculate Western style three piece suit correct upto the pocket-kerchief and the button flower, as Apu reads a patriotic poem for him during the inspection visit.(APJT 39)

In AS, you hear the PP Theme tune once while Apu describes to Pulu the almost autobiographical novel where his main character is a priest's son who rejects the family tradition for seeking new sources of life in the city (AS 18).

From the design point of view, several other uses of background music are interesting. One late night Indir sings in her tired old voice of the evening gloom increasing around as this pauper prays for divine help in crossing the river when she is incapable of paying the boat hire. The song is spread over this silently suffering household, Harihar and Sarbojaya and herself, but it avoids the children who have already slept before Indir starts singing (PP-18). The song is repeated over **the scene of Indir's own funeral sung in her own voice since no other voice can take on the moral value of this tired, cracked voice** (PP-23-24). An early scene when Indir is introduced eating her morning gruel, with little Durga waiting behind has a background tarshenai playing the tune of the song (PP-3). The tune also accompanies Indir as she goes out begging for shelter in Raju's house (PP19).

Consider another **example of music across the films**. In APJT, Harihar died suddenly, quite unexpectedly, even as he was just about settling down. Recall the visual composition. As the sacred water is poured in his mouth, his eyes bulge out in death. We hear Sarbojaya's startled cry "Ki Holo?" (What has happened?) as a sudden release which is continued visually on a flock of ghat pigeons take off and circle around in the open sky. The human cry also triggers off a high flute tune in Rag Jog accompanied by string vibrations which continue and get spent over the next two shots showing Apu in the ten day post-funeral rituals on the riverside (APJT-18). Let us call this music piece Harihar's Death Tune. (For shape of this tune see Index on Music). On his first visit home from Calcutta Apu is telling Sarbojaya of the places he has seen. When the list goes on from Kalighat to Keortala, the burning ghat, the background music takes on the Harihar Death Tune (APJT-66). Sarobjaya is disturbed by Apu's reference to Keortola, and she breaks off sharply cautioning Apu that he should be careful on the roads in Calcutta. In a much later scene, the Tune appears again on Sarbojaya as she hallucinates that Apu has returned to her (APJT-78), while she lingers to a slow death as the poolside fireflies dance and the distant animals howl. In AS, when Apu interacts with Pulu and forces himself to talk of Aparna's death, Harihar's death music reappears (AS-69) as if quoting the suddenness of the event and helplessness of the situation.

Think of the **example connecting PP and AS**. We have used it earlier but it will bear repetition here. In PP, Sarbojaya had contained herself after Durga's death up to the moment when Harihar shows the sari he has brought for Durga. This is when Sarbojaya breaks out in a wail. Visually we see her cry, but do not hear the sound. Instead we hear a tune of high notes (Raga Patdeep) on tarshenai which is named **Mother's Wail** (PP-36)for convenience of reference. This music covers Harihar's initial shock as he starts getting up to move away, but corrects fast by bringing his body down for making a physical contact with Sarbojaya. The tune moves on to cover Apu who is coming back home but halts before venturing further towards the house. Mother's Wail is used again at the end of AS in the crucial segment of the conciliation scene between Kajal and Apu. Apu had failed in his prolonged attempt to connect with his son Kajal. He was leaving, moving away along the river bank. From a distance Kajal sees him go away, and Apu halts. There is a short verbal interchange in which Apu is recognised as a "friend" who will take Kajal to his "father" in Calcutta. In the meanwhile Grandfather also comes calling out for Kajal. Apu beckons Kajal as he runs towards him. **Mother's Wail music covers Apu and Kajal's run towards him (AS-81).** At the end of the run, Apu picks up Kajal on his shoulders and the very triumphant title music takes over as they move on triumphantly to the end of the film.

For detailed comment, see Introduction where this music is analysed for density of expression.

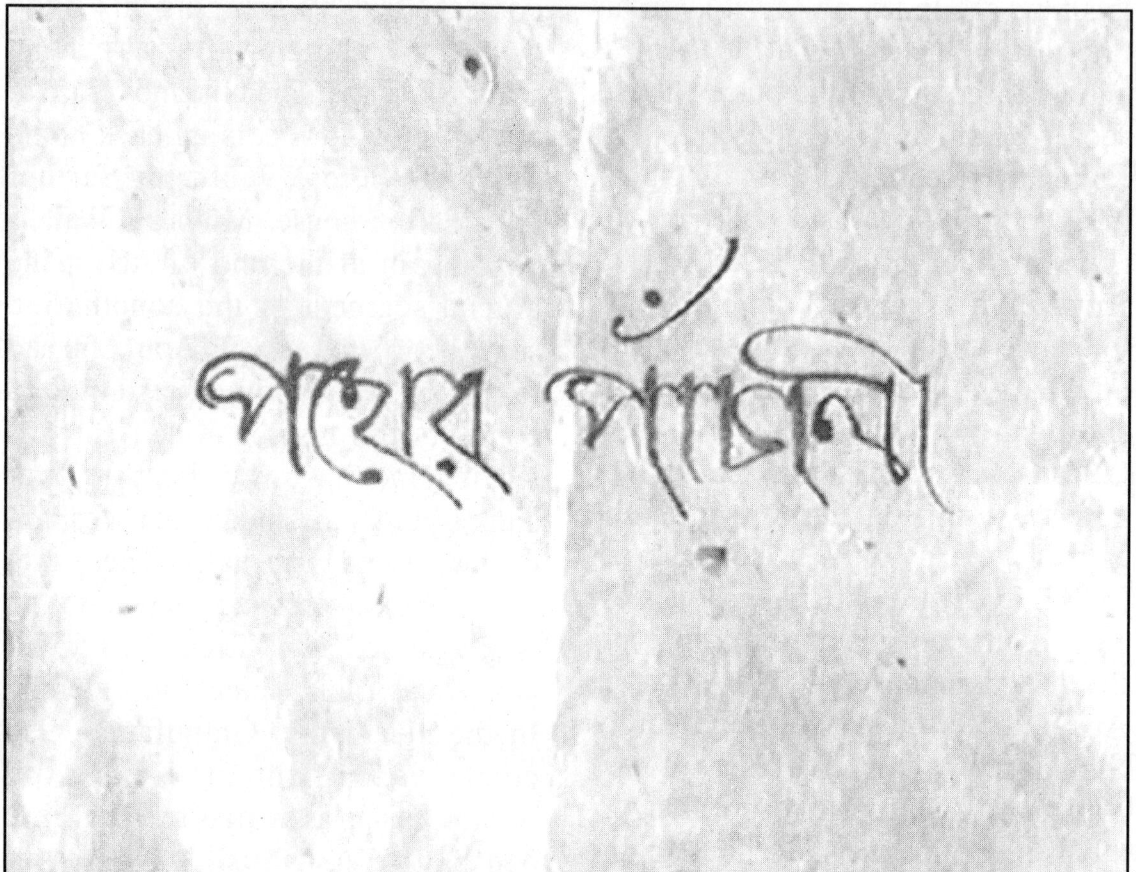

Credit Still Pather Panchali

Chapter 3

TEXTUAL ANALYSIS OF THE THREE FILMS

The Apu Trilogy exhibits a strong rhythm of three in its structure. In all the three films the narration has a structure with a convenient three part division. Each part is also structured to exhibit three segments in it. We are using a numbering system for identifying different elements in the film. In the study of design in the films, we will constantly have to refer to elements which should be identified by a referencing system. Forward and backward reference to details of films will constantly be made as we proceed with the analysis.

The concepts for understanding the Film medium presented in the previous chapters will be used for exploring the Trilogy as a whole. This chapter would include a description of the content of what we see and hear from the film on screen followed by some analytical comments relevant to the structure and design aspects of the film.The description of the film will very often merge with the comments as a part of the stylistics of analysis here.

Throughout the films of the Trilogy, the visual evidence of literacy, handwritten letters, printed material, signboards, scribblings and graffiti on the walls, such elements are observed by the camera and consistently used in composition. Surely, this is a trivial detail. However, in an incremental art like film, the trivial details accumulate and create the visual-social textures against which the human drama unfolds. Thus, from the very opening of PP, with the unfolding of Apu's life the theme of education is consciously used in numerous background details of film composition.

PATHER PANCHALI

The style of calligraphy of the credit titles of the three films of the Trilogy follows a design suggested by the themes of literacy and scholarship in the films. The credit titles of PP are written in ornamental Bengali calligraphy by a reed pen on textured handmade papersheet which has a vertical dent casued by a fold in an old manuscript. The professional mode of Harihar's ancestral family is

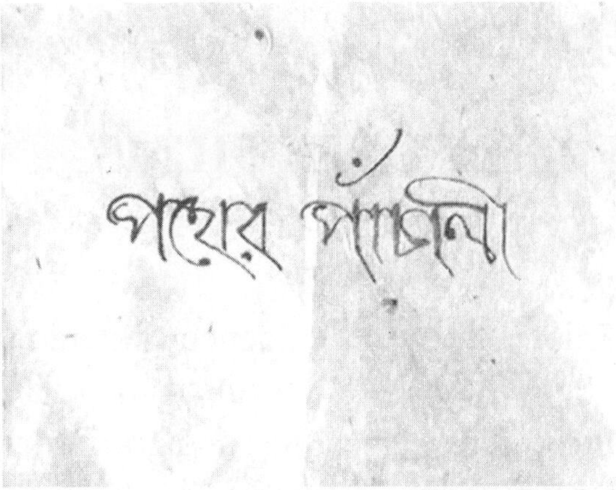

Pather Panchali

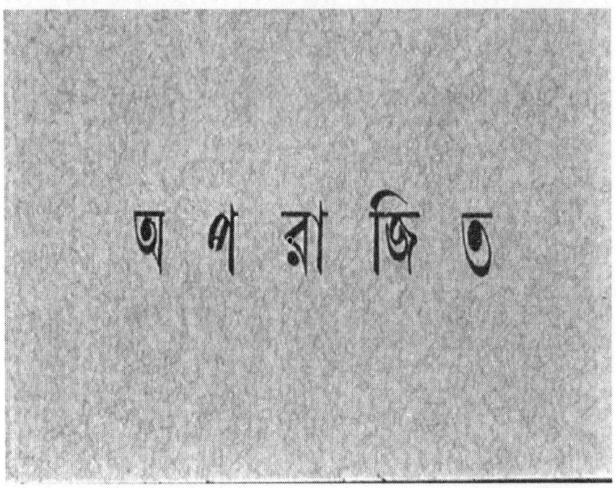

Aparajito

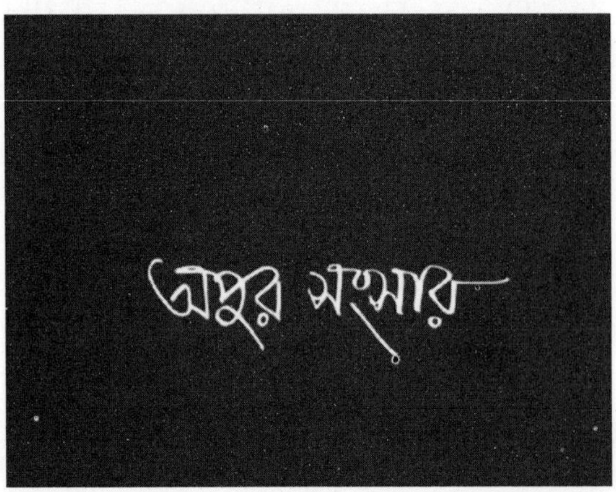

Apur Sansar

scholarship. Harihar himself is trying to sustain himself as a scholarly priest and also hoping to supplement it with more secular writing of jatra plays. When Harihar is leaving the village, he is shown packing up some old manuscripts.

In APJT Apu has moved to the level of the printed book which is above Harihar's manuscript level. Hence the titles of APJT are written in the visual style of book print. In AS Apu is already a writer. The titles of AS are free flowing hadwriting of an educated person.

This sense of design also occurs in the music track of the titles segment in PP, based mainly on Rag Khamaj. There are four musical tunes in the title music: (i) The drums (ii) A happy tune played on sitar (iii) The PP theme tune and (iv) a vibrato. (For details see Index on Music.) Each one of these is associated with some special mood of the event in the plot. It starts off with a drum *tihai* played on *pakhavaj*. *Drums* are culturally associated with the *raudra* mood, the anger of authority. In the film it is associated with scenes which show moods of anger. The second tune is a happy lilting tune on sitar, let us call it the Happy Tune and it is associated with happy, light moods in the film. The third tune played on flute is the PP

Theme Tune, has become well known since its variations have been released in recordings by Ravi Shankar, the music director of the film. It is associated with events which are crucial in the lives of these characters, and it has been used in APJT and AS as well. Hence the PP Theme Tune also acts as to bind the three films. The fourth tune is a vibrato, a single note vibrating in a repetitive manner which is first heard in the background of the ending the PP tune in the title music. The vibrato with several variations is associated with situations of suffering, of separation of characters.

In PP and the Trilogy, background musical tunes which are associated with moods are carefully used in the design of the plot.

PP shows why Apu's father, Harihar Ray abandoned his ancestral village and moved to Benares. The narrative is developed in three stages as follows.

PP-1: Harihar struggles to live in the ancestral village, and goes out for some time.

PP-2: Harihar is away temporarily. The family is under severe strain.

PP-3: Harihar finally abandons the village home.

The first part PP-1 is large and for handling the analysis, we will break it up in three segments PP-1 Seg 1, PP-1 Seg 2 and PP-1 Seg 3. Each of these segments are also large and can be divided into three subsegments. Thus for analytical purposes PP-1 will have nine subsegments. While in the description of segments and subsegments we will indicate these divisions, we will number them continuously from PP 1.1 to PP 1.9. This exception is being made purely for the convenience of referencing.

The first part of PP-1 Seg 1 has the following subsegments:

PP-1.1: The Guava Stealing Episode

PP-1.2: Apu is born

PP-1.3: Dreams of the family

We will now look at these subsegments in detail.

PP- 1.1 Guava Stealing Episode

It is morning on Shejobou's terrace. After her bath, she is spreading out the washing. As she offers prayers to a *tulsi* plant she notices Durga pilfering fruit in orchard below. Shejobou shouts Durga away. As Durga runs, the patter of her feet is heard. Durga moves smartly homewards in the bamboo grove path, away from Shejobou's scolding. A snatch of music comes on and stops as Durga notices Sarbojaya coming up on her way to the water well in Shejobou's courtyard. Durga withdraws cautiously aside and hides till Sarbojaya has safely crossed her. The background music is resumed as Durga briskly moves homeward, moving past the cow which has been milked, enters the door and goes straight to Indir's verandah. Indir is not in. Durga puts one guava in Indir's fruit pot and picks up its covering dish. Moving to the kitchen verandah she fills the dish with milk from the pot. Then she moves to the corner of the courtyard to feed her pet kitten. Durga's smiling face is framed in the circular mouth of the large pot in which the kitten is kept. She takes the kitten out and starts feeding it milk from the dish.

A woman from a nearby balcony reacts to Shejobou saying that the child's misbehaviour is a trivial matter and could be referred to the mother for correction. In the meanwhile, Sarbojaya enters Shejobou's courtyard for drawing water from the well. Shejobou moves on the terrace to position herself to shout at Sarbojaya down below, making the unfair accusation that it is the mother who is encouraging the child to steal. Nilmoni's Wife is also at the well. Sarbojaya refuses her help to carry the heavy pot. Nilmoni's Wife looks with disapproval towards Shejobou's terrace.

In Harihar's house, old Indir is eating gruel from a bowl. Durga sits quietly behind. In the background we hear on dilruba the tune of a song that Indir will sing one night much later. Indir becomes aware of Durga only after she has finished eating, and she feels sorry about not being able to give some food to Durga. Indir now notices Durga's gift of the pilfered guava, and both enjoy this moment of discovery. However, Sarbojaya is now back home from the well. Sarbojaya does not like Durga sitting close to Indir when she is eating and asks them to separate. Durga makes a momentary childlike resistance. When Sarbojaya repeats her order, Indir defends Durga by saying that the child was not bothering her at all. However, she also persuades her to go when mother calls. Sarbojaya asks Durga to go back and return the pilfered guavas to Shejobou. Durga goes out as ordered by the mother.

After the meal Indir rinses her mouth, and uses the leftover water in the pot to water a plant. Indir annoys the already upset Sarbojaya by dusting her rags. Sarbojaya accuses Indir that she is inciting Durga to steal fruit. Indir defends the act of pilfering fruit as a mere child's prank, and the accusation that she is spoiling Durga is mere nonsense. Sarbojaya feels slighted at this. She shifts the accusation to Indir's own habit of pilfering salt, oil and chillies from Sarbojaya's kitchen. She threatens to turn Indir out of the house if she persists in spoiling the child. Indir gets really angry at this and starts packing her rags. Indir throws her bundle of rags which lands on a kitten, who is cursed and pushed out of the way. A tune played on majira cymbals is the background music to Indir's departure from the house. Indir collects all her stuff and moves out towards the door without responding to Sarbojaya's query about where she is going. Out in the lane, Durga, returning from Shejobou's house, makes a childlike attempt to stop her, but the determined Indir brushes her aside. Durga is also called away inside the house by Sarbojaya. PP theme music begins and covers Durga as she is put on to sweeping the courtyard upto fade out.

The opening scene introduces the women characters from the immediate social environment in which Apu is born. They interact around Durga pilfering fruit. This brings out norms of behaviour and parenting shared by these women. Shejobou's objection may seem overdone, as the neighbour tries to point out. The accusation on Durga is flung on to Sarbojaya who in turn takes it home and passes it on to old Indir. The final outcome of the whole episode is that Indir leaves the house in anger and Durga is corrected and put to household chores. These scenes use the morning routine of the women in a pattern of living. The bickerings would also be part of the pattern. Some positive norms of social interaction are also established. The well within Shejobou's compound is open for the other women of the community and Nilmoni's Wife is using the well by this custom. Nilmoni's Wife is sympathetic towards Sarbojaya whereas Shejobou is indifferent to her.Durga is a child.Others tend to take a more lenient view of her misbehaviour. Sarbojaya however wants to correct her and insists upon returning the fruit she had pilfered.

Compositionally, when Shejobou is accusing Sarbojaya, the camera leaves Shejobou and the words fall on Sarbojaya's face and body. Likewise when Sarbojaya accuses Indir, the words fall on Indir's face and body as she moves away.

Shejobou, Durga and Sarbojaya are connected by three lines of tension which form a triangular relationship. Shejobou shouting Durga away from the fruit trees creates a line of tension. Shejobou's accusation causes another line of tension between her and Sarbojaya. Despite this Sarbojaya shares with Shejobou in the norm that a child should not steal. Sarbojaya and Durga form another line created by the complex mother and daughter relationship. Sarbojaya needs to bring up Durga with correct norms. However there is also a leniency standard which may vary at adult discretion.

Sarbojaya, Durga and Indir are also presented in a triangular relationship. There is a positive bond between Durga and Indir. The Sarbojaya-Indir relationship is negatively charged for two reasons: Indir has attached herself to the family by some distant relationship and she encourages the flouting of norms that Sarbojaya wants Durga to learn and follow. In this incident, Durga's pilfering fruit may be a trivial matter, but Sarbojaya's personal pride is hurt by the verbal lashing from Shejobou. The manner in which the verbal lashing is administered by Sarbojaya on Indir is similar to the manner she has received it from Shejobou. The dynamics of this triangle causes the movement of the narrative as Indir leaves the house. The mother continues training the daughter in household skills when she asks Durga to sweep the courtyard.

This working of the triangles is softened by nuances like motherly protectiveness, and also by the convincing manner in which the children's world is created within the adult world. Durga has a little corner to herself in which the pet cat and kitten can be kept and fed on the milk drawn from the household stock.

A pattern of triangular relationships of subtle tensions between these characters is initiated here and it will continue to operate through the film. The triangles will push the narrative along the lines of conflict and their resolution.

Thematically, survival with dignity is a central issue which is threatened by Shejobou by branding a mere childish prank as stealing caused by bad upbringing by the mother. Indir's anger on the other hand is triggered off by a similar sense of dignity, even though she has a dependent status in this household. In terms of design, the Shejobou-Sarbojaya-Durga triangle will repeat in the necklace stealing episode.In the ending scenes of the film the triangularity will be resolved when Shejobou brings a gift of fruit when Sarbojaya is packing to leave the village.

The details of the environment are built in carefully. The general ambience of trees and greenery, the path along the pond which connects the two houses, the details of Harihar's house, the door and the path outside it will be used in the visual composition repeatedly and with consistency.These elements will enter the design of narration.

PP 1.2 Apu is Born

Apu's birth is done in three short movements. First we see Durga asleep, while Harihar, the anxious father paces the verandah. In the delivery hut, Shejobou sits a little distant chewing a pan while Nilmoni's Wife comforts Sarbojaya in labour pain. Back to the anxious Harihar dissolve to close up of Sarbojaya's face in pain. Dissolve to next morning. Durga comes along with Indir returning home on this happy occasion. As Indir enters the door she is greeted by a neighbour woman who is moving out with a pot to get the daily household supply of water from the well. The courtyard is crowded with women and children who have come to greet the birth of the baby boy. Durga puts Indir's bundles in the corner of her hut while Indir herself goes on to see Sarbojaya and the newborn baby. Sarbojaya does not smile as she shows the baby's face to them. Durga and Indir, both smile looking at the lovable infant. Durga continues to smile while Indir wipes a tear of joy.

The Apu Trilogy is about Apu. It is therefore logical that the film starts around the time of Apu's birth. Even though Apu is a child in PP, the action of the adults is eventually around Apu. The narrative will make more sense if we consider Harihar and Sarbojaya as Apu's parents and Durga as Apu's sister.

Notice the configuration of characters in this sequence. The newly born Apu is at the centre, and around him is a circular movement of caring people, the coming together of the family, of the neighbours and the community. The birth of a son in this family is also a joyous event for other families of the community.

This coming-together feeling of this sequence balances the moving-away quality of the first segment (PP 1.1) which had the tone of quarrels and disapprovals and dominant triangular interactions. With the occasion of joy for the family, the strain between Sarbojaya and Indir softens as the old woman returns and Sarbojaya accommodates her. Indir would definitely be a help under the circumstances of the family. The simultaneous existence of such opposite elements in characters comes from a deeper understanding of patterns of human relationships.

When they return, Indir and Durga are seen at the same spot in the lane where they had parted in the previous scene. An angry Indir had strained away, now she is drawn by the happy news towards the house. Sarbojaya gives an uncertain reception to Indir when she asks her to let her see the child's face. Indir and Durga are at the two ends of the life cycle, but they have the strong bond of the very old and the very young. They also share certain other characteristics. They do not care about strict observance of the norms, they are delighted by the infant Apu, and visually, both are toothless!

PP 1.3 Dreams of the Family

Five months have passed since Apu's birth. Now we come to a scene which indicates the pattern of aspirations of Harihar's life. The scene opens with a side view of Apu in an improvised swing being rocked by Indir singing a lullaby. Durga plays by counting dried seeds. Then the camera leaves them and moves into the kitchen where Harihar and Sarbojaya talk about the good omen of Apu's arrival and of the plan of a possible community feast to celebrate the first grain-feeding ceremony, when Sarbojaya's cooking skills would be praised by the guests. Harihar has been promised a job in the landowner's office next month. Sarbojaya is apprehensive if he will be paid regularly. Harihar is optimistic, with faith in the goodness of the employer. Sarbojaya points out Harihar's gullibility in the manner in which their fruit trees were taken away by Shejobou's people under the pretext of settling an unrecorded debt of a generation ago. Harihar counters with the hopeful dream that he would be writing new plays which would be liked more than the current productions and that will bring in money. Sarbojaya is relieved at the prospect that Harihar would be respected as a learned person. Together, they talk about their future responsibilities like Apu's education and Durga's marriage. They feel confident that there would be enough for a simple living of two meals a day and a few new clothes once in the year. The scene comes full circle back to Indir and Apu. The camera tilts down from Indir's face on to the infant Apu in the swing. The stills from this scene have be shown in an earlier reference.

The circular shape of this scene moves around to include the core concerns of the family, the acceptance of their present state of affairs, and their dreams for the future. The camera view shifts from Apu's swing to Durga's little toybox on to the kitchen verandah. Indir is back with a functional place in the family. However, the relationships are getting more complex. Durga has a little baby brother, who is much too small just now, but soon he would grow up to be an accomplice, a ward and even a small boy to be bossed over. Harihar Ray is a priest in the traditional mode, like his ancestors who were also reputed for high learning. However, times have changed. Harihar is a non-assertive, gullible person and he has lost some land and fruit trees in settling the doubtful loan of a kin of earlier generation. Sarbojaya is worried at his weak role as provider of the family and his daydreaming. He is willing to work in the landlord's office for a while, not indefinitely. He imagines that he would write original poetry and plots in jatra plays, which would be popular with the players, and this would bring him money and also fame as a writer. Apu's father is contrasted with the mother Sarbojaya. This strong woman is aware of imminent dangers and tries to make careful provision for eventualities. The concerns of the family are articulated here in terms of Apu's education and Durga's marriage and the repairs of the house. Apu's parents are aspiring for a simple life of survival with dignity. The film shows how even these modest aspirations would not work out for the family and why Harihar Ray has eventually to abandon the ancestral village and migrate to Benares.

This scene has a circular shape since it begins with Apu in cradle and ends with him after moving around the others emphasising the togetherness of the family while stating their major binding concerns of what would follow in the story. The Trilogy will follow with detailed scenes expressive of themes stated in this scene like the education of the son, a daughter's marriage (Ranu instead of Durga) and repair to the house which will not happen, and the continuing inefficacy of Harihar as the breadwinner while Sarbojaya's struggles to keep the family going.

The next section of the film opens when Apu is six years old. The pattern of living of Apu's family repeats with some variations even while its economic condition continues to be fragile. However, as Apu grows up, he learns from the many events in the expanding physical and social circle of the community around him.

The Pattern Six Years Later

This is the second segment of the first part. It has three subsegments as follows:

PP-1.4: Apu goes to school

PP-1.5: The necklace stealing episode, and

PP-1.6: Dreams of the future persist.

PP- 1.4 Apu Goes to School

It begins one morning, but there is a difference. Sarbojaya comes in with some firewood and asks Durga to wake up Apu as he starts schooling today. The milkmaid comments that the cow is not being fed properly, since the quantity of milk yield has reduced. Durga wakes up Apu in a playful interaction. He cleans his teeth. Sarbojaya and Durga dress him up for the school. Apu drinks a bowl of milk. All the while Indir is seen carrying on her routine. Durga escorts Apu to the school. The PP Theme tune comes on. A village elder notices the children as they pass by.

Apu's school is in an extention of a grocery shop where the students sit on the floor below the verandah where Prosanna the shopkeeper sells his wares and also at the same time teaches. The shop is also a meeting place for the villagers. Prosanna dictates a high flown literary passage to the children to write on their slates, and simultaneously strikes up a conversation with Baidya Muzumdar, a village elder. Apu smiles at a joke when the nine school kids are referred to as Navaratna (nine gems), and he is admonished for the smile. Their conversation moves on to discuss the forthcoming Puja festival, and the excellent drummers they have hired for the occasion. Prosanna notices the children playing naughts and crosses on their slate instead of writing. He singles out the erring boy for punishment with heavy caning. Apu winces with the sound as the cane strikes the erring boy. Puti, a little girl who had come to buy puffed rice, runs away from the caning as fast as she can.

The pattern after six years begins with the morning routine, and with the opening up of Apu's world through the school. Indir has not changed, but Durga has grown up, smarter and much in accordance with the mother's expectations. Sarbojaya is busy in her morning routine which keeps the family going, including going out with the pots for the household supply of water from the well. When Apu is woken up his eye is first seen through the hole in his chadar. There are several visual compositions that have a circular motif. Earlier we have seen Durga's face framed by the opening of the pot. This was part of Durga's world within the adult world. Apu's eye seen through the hole is part of the childhood fun as well as the indication of the torn chadar. Later we will see Indir requesting Harihar for a new chadar looking at him through the big hole in her chadar. Her appeal is made stronger, more

urgent by the visual composition. As Apu drinks milk, the circular shape of the bowl covering his face is repeated in the scene when Sarbojaya refuses shelter to Indir. In APJT it will occur when Harihar has a bowl of milk with cream for him. In each case the circle suggests different nuances of meaning. Very much later in AS we will see Aparna's face framed through a hole in the curtain in Apu's room.

Preparing Apu for school is portrayed with joy and loving care. He is the centre of attention and admiration. Look at the composition in which the mother and sister are preparing Apu that morning. It reflects several aspects of the importance of the male child in the family.

Sarbojaya's face has the look of a mother watching the son grown up enough for going to school, which is a matter of good luck for her. This kind of training for Durga in simple acts like combing his hair is also an aspect of her special love for younger brother.

Later in the film after Durga's death, when Apu cleans his teeth and combs his hair, the repetition of action in the earlier scenes is designed to probe the emotional depth in simple everyday relationship of a brother and sister.

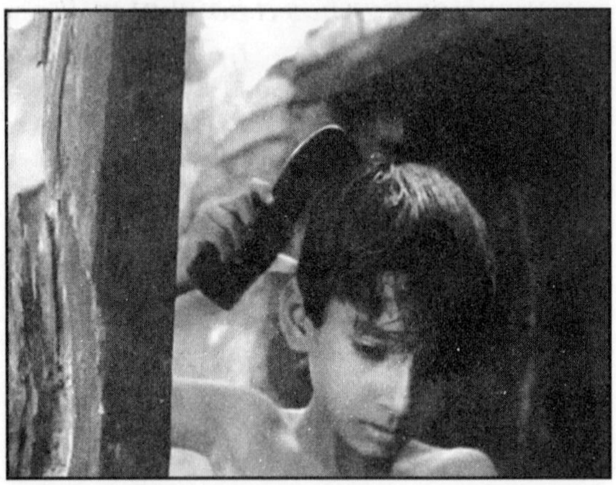

Apu's school is full of details that bring out the quality of life in the village and the level of education possible here.The teacher's dictation has no pedagogical thought. The passage for dictation is interesting for the rhythmic beauty of the language. They are, in fact, lines from a master, Iswarchandra Vidyasagar, but they are well above the comprehension of the children. However, here it does not matter, since the boys find their own ways of amusing themselves until they are caught by the teacher. The children are supposed to obey the teacher and the errant boy is heavily punished. This is Apu's first experience of violence.

The teacher's main concern is to supplement the income from the shop

and to provide a centre for the village gossip. The little adjustments are struck in undertone by the shopkeeper and Muzumdar. The children are not supposed to hear it! The adult world is very different from the child's world.

This is the first school in the Trilogy.The girl child is not a part of it. The little girl who looks at the school with curiosity is pushed away by the punishment. In APJT we see another school run under the system that controls the syllabi and monitors the educational practice. Apu's college in Calcutta is run by the same system at a higher level.We also have some levels of teaching outside the schools. One night, Harihar will be giving some interesting words for Apu to write on his slate. In APJT Apu is learning some English from his friends. In AS the teaching in the family continues when Apu explains some English words to Aparna.

Notice the rhythmic pattern of the emotional tones of scenes. The opening had the tensions, followed by the circular coming together at the time of Apu's birth. The family circle continued into the dreams of the family with a little difference of viewpoint between Apu's mother and father. Now, six years later, the care and adulation that Apu receives has the happy tone, the school dictation has the concentration of children learning to write and a bit of humour created by the gossip centre aspect of the location. The school scene ends in the tension created by the severe punishment given to the erring student.The sounds of the caning fall on Apu's face and the little girl running away.

PP 1.5 The Necklace Stealing Episode

It is noon time. Indir takes some chillies from Sarbojaya's kitchen. Sarbojaya admonishes her for it. Durga comes in with the stolen fruit she habitually gets for Indir's enjoyment. Sarbojaya calls Durga and asks her to clean the vegetables and talks about the duties of a growing girl and all the things she needs to learn. She checks Durga's forehead for temperature and advises her to take the *tulsi* leaf juice.

This scene works out the details of Sarbojaya's issues with Indir. In the earlier scene she had accused Indir of encouraging Durga to pilfer fruit and of her pilfering from Sarbojaya's kitchen. Six years have passed but both continue to pilfer. However, Durga has grown smarter. She continues to pilfer fruit for Indir but follows mother's instructions in her training as well. Sarbojaya is concerned about Durga's health since she has a tendency to run fever in the evenings.

This section confirms Durga's tendency to satisfy her needs by methods disapproved by norms of good behaviour she is expected to acquire. It also has a complex evening scene which introduces several strands of developments that occur later.

Harihar comes home with Apu. Apu runs upto mother asking for something to eat, trying to touch the edge of her sari where she knots in coins. Sarbojaya is cooking and she asks Apu not to touch her. Apu could have some puffed rice in the big bowl. Durga could take it out for him. Harihar notices Indir who has to be helped to get up to her verandah. She shows her torn chadar and Harihar promises to buy one for her. Durga calls Apu in her corner as she makes a tasty pickle-like concoction with raw mangoes and oil. Durga asks Apu to ensure that mother should not know about this pickle making.

This little scene shows growing demands on Harihar. Children find a way of eating something as they wait for the meal. Indir's chadar is badly torn and Harihar promises to buy one for her. Sarbojaya overhears and looks a little annoyed by Harihar's promise.

The strain on the lives of the adults does not affect the children. They improvise in the making of the pickle, and enjoy keeping this secret as an adventure of their own which mother does not know about. They will enjoy such private thrills later in the film when they run out to the far distant meadow of the telegraph poles and the railway track, and also when they drench in the rain.

While tasting the sour pickle, the children hear the tinkling of the sweetseller's bells. The sweetseller calls out the names of the delicacies he is offering. Apu tries to get a pice from Harihar who is willing but Sarbojaya intervenes. She asks Harihar not to give any money to the children. Durga, however, does not give up. The children follow the sweetseller to Shejobou's house. Durga joins the group of playing children and Apu halts outside the gate.A boy teases him. Shejobou has bought from the sweetseller and she resents Durga coming in at this time. Durga mixes with her friends and goes up on the terrace of the house. Tunu is sitting there stringing beads. Durga wants to try stringing the beads herself, but Tunu refuses. Ranu also comes upstairs with a sweet that she has pilfered and gives it to Durga.

The little desires of children in a poor household are being set aside. They are hungry and the sweetseller has enticed them calling out a long list of delicacies. However, they do not get the coin. Father seems to be ready to give the coin, but Mother prevents him. Every coin has to be carefully spent in this household The children decide to follow the sweetseller to Shejobou's house. The walk is visually done in terms of the sweetseller with swinging pots followed by the children and the dog in trail, and later the geese joining in. The little procession is reflected in the placid pool. Lively music accompanies the sweetseller's little procession. Durga goes in but Apu keeps out.

Shejobou does not like Durga's presence when they are buying sweets. However, Durga has joined the playing group and moves on to the terrace. Ranu defies Shejobou and pilfers a sweet and brings it up for Durga. Ranu's stolen beads will carry the story forward, and ultimately be discovered by Apu and consigned to the depths of this very pond.

Shejobou is now dressed in a widow's white sari. A death is being reported in the film narrative by visual means.

This is followed by a complex evening scene.The children bring the cow to the shed. Sarbojaya lights a lamp at the tulsi plant, Indir offers her prayers. With rituals going on in other houses, we hear the conch sound. Darkness swiftly covers the banana groves. In the night sequence, Harihar is writing a horoscope for some client. He is also asking Apu to practice writing some words on his slate. Indir brings out a bundle of clothes. Durga sits by, Sarbojaya separates them. She calls her for doing her hair. She slaps her lightly. They sit near Apu and Harihar. On her verandah Indir tries to thread a needle to repair the hole in her chadar, checking if she could draw Harihar's attention for reminder of his promise. The small conversation within the family moves around Ranu's marriage and Durga's desire to make her hair with four strands which is not possible in the dry condition of her hair The distant train whistle is heard and the children talk about going to see the train some day. Harihar interacts playfully with Apu as he asks him to write the word "ghost".

This is a scene in which nothing seems to happen but it is rich with suggestions of future events. Ranu's marriage will be worked out in detail. The children will see the train one day. Indir's chadar will involve her in a fateful quarrel with Sarbojaya. And Apu's education will be a major concern running through PP and APJT. The scene brings together several strands of the narrative even while portraying the slow pattern of life of this family.

The next scene shows Sarbojaya feeding Apu while the dog waits around. Apu is however intent on playing around with an improvised bow and arrow. She asks if he has studied properly and is not bullied in the school. Apu is however involved in his play and refuses to eat anymore. Sarbojaya gives the rice away to feed the dog, while grumbling that uninteresting food like rice and potato every day could not possibly be relished by Apu.

As Apu tries to run out, the door of the house opens suddenly and an aggressive Shejobou enters accompanied by Tunu and other girls. Durga is being accused of stealing Tunu's bead necklace, and further Sarbojaya is accused of training Durga in stealing. Durga's toybox is ruthlessly searched and nothing is found. An argument ensues, and Sarbojaya is badly slighted. Durga is around, Apu tries to wave her away, but mother calls her in. Sarbojaya prevents Shejobou from touching Durga, but she herself searches Durga and nothing is found on her except some dried kernels. Even these, Shejobou claims are from her orchard. Shejobou leaves, hurling insults, asking for immediate repayment of some five rupees Sarbojaya had borrowed from her sometime, also ensuring that a neighbourhood woman in the lane also listens to her accusations. A very angry Sarbojaya now punishes Durga, dragging her by the hair and throwing her out of the house. Having done that Sarbojaya is exhausted and sits down huddled at the door crying softly to herself. Apu has watched all this outburst of violence. He settles down to read aloud from a schoolbook, which is all he can do to please the mother. Indir also tries to help by putting back the scattered bits into Durga's toybox and taking the clothing off the line. After a while, Sarbojaya composes herself and asks Apu to go out and search for Durga and get her home for her meal.

We now see Sarbojaya rearing her children. She is asking Apu about the school to ensure that he has no problems there. His loss of interest in eating is ascribed to the repetition of rice and potato in every meal. The practice of feeding a grown up child so that he eats well is an aspect of rearing that makes the son of the family dependent on adults in selfmanage-ment and general grooming. We can see this in APJT when Apu is hardly able to pack for himself when going to Calcutta.

The triangular interaction between Shejobou, Durga and

Sarbojaya reaches a peak in this scene. To foil Shejobou's accusation, Sarbojaya joins in searching Durga with a dual purpose of proving that Durga is not likely to steal anything that costs money, and that she is serious about punishing Durga. To her relief, nothing is found on Durga's person or her belongings, but the sharp reminder to return some borrowed money triggers off her anger for punishing Durga. Apu's second exposure to violence is an intense experience since it occurs in an otherwise comforting context. Durga is being punished, not for anything she has stolen. It is rather for Sarbojaya's humiliation that Durga has earned for herself a reputation of a thief. The visuals of Durga's punishment are accompanied by the sound of a drum on the sound track. Culturally, drums are associated with anger and violence.The blows are not seen, but we see Apu wincing. Towards the end of the film when Apu discovers that the necklace was actually stolen by Durga, and she had told him a lie, Apu decides to keep the dead sister's secret by throwing the necklace into the pond, the drum music of the punishment scene is repeated on Apu's face and body, as a reminder of Durga being punished.

The necklace stealing episode starts with a circular protective scene between Apu and mother. It is followed immediately by the sharp lines of Shejobou-Durga-Sarbojaya triangularities, leading to severe punishment for Durga, and again a circular scene of Indir and Apu trying to help Sarbojaya till she calms down and asks Apu to get Durga back for her meal. Apu remains, most of the time an observer of the way events occur.This entire complicated scene begins with Apu and ends with Apu, even though he is a mere observer of what is happening.

Sarbojaya upholds the norm that the reputation of the family should not be tarnished in any manner. Durga gets punished for doing that. Likewise, with Indir, who will get thrown out of the house precisely because she begged for the chadar from an outsider, thereby indicating to the community that Harihar is a bad provider for the family.

The strain on the pattern of life begins to show in routine physical things, like the quantity of milk yielded by the cow gets reduced since she is not being fed adequately, or Indir's chadar gets torn and needs immediate replacement. Durga, in her state of deprivation, is not able to observe norms of self-control, though this is what she is expected to learn.

PP 1.6 Dreams of the Future Persist

Indir tells a horror story to the children. Harihar comes in with good news: he has received his salary arrears. He has bought fish for dinner. Sarbojaya is slow to respond. She is under strain of the insulting events earlier in the day. She receives the purse containing coins of the salary. As Harihar eats, he talks of prospects at getting a client in Dashghora. She has her worries and reservations. Harihar tries to alleviate her anxiety. However, she talks about the money to be paid to Shejobou.

Apu and Durga run up to the verandah and go to bed. Apu asks Durga in confidence about the stolen necklace. She denies that she stole it, and says that she does not know who did.

Harihar and Sarbojaya talk as he lies down to sleep and she sits aside working on repairing some old clothes. Harihar talks about a new plot of a play he is planning to write. Sarbojaya suggests that they might go to Benares for a better living, an idea which Harihar readily rejects, since he does not want to leave this ancestral village. Sarbojaya talks of how her dreams of doing this and that have all been frustrated. However, Harihar is not listening. He has slept off.

Indir's song comes on this background. She sits in the darkness of her verandah, and sings softly in her tired rusted voice a request to the divine boatman to take her across the river of life. It is evening, and this pauper has no means to pay for the crossing…

As soon as the strain is temporarily relieved, the dreams return with full force and the worries get deeper. Apu had started growing with a critical sense and started asking the crucial question from Durga. She is hardening in her defiance of the norms of good behaviour which apply when your basic needs are met. She flatly denies that she stole the bead necklace and she does not know who stole it. Harihar continues to be naïvely optimistic. Sarbojaya continues to be isolated, since Harihar does not even consider her suggestion of change, and is already asleep when she talks of her own dreams.

Indir's relevance to the family is seen largely in terms of children. Now that they are grown up, she tells them stories in the night. This horror story links at the feeling level with Sarbojaya's apprehensions, of imminent danger. Indir's song is about her dispossessed status and the need for divine grace to carry her across with dignity.

In the earlier scene dealing with the dreams of the family, the movement was from a lullaby for the baby Apu, moving around to the sister and the parents and end up with the lullaby for Apu. Here it starts with a story of horror, goes around the family to a song praying for taking the soul across the river of life. Both the scenes have a circular shape and they examine the inner core of the family. They begin at the outer part, Indir and move through the core and get back to Indir. The first scene had isolation and togetherness of Sarbojaya and Harihar, in the second, Apu is isolated from Durga from a position of togetherness as he asks the critical question. In both cases Sarbojaya is weighed down by the worries and imminent dangers. Harihar continues to be the simple optimistic self. Sarbojaya's fears come true in the course of the film and Harihar has to leave the ancestral abode in search of survival with dignity. The third section of the film is entirely devoted to the undoing of these dreams.

Pattern of Harihar's Life Starts Cracking up

The narrative in this third segment of PP 1 is divided into three subsegments

PP-1.7: (a)chadar begging episode intercut with (b) picnic scene

PP-1.8: (a) puja-jatra (b) children discover train,intercut with (c) Indir's death

PP-1.9: Harihar leaves to earn more money

The pattern we have seen laid out in the first segment was already under some strain in the second segment and as the burdens increase, it starts cracking up. The children's world widens in all directions, and the adult world serves as a symbiotic background for it. As individuals hold on, the community stays intact.

Durga and the other children have a picnic. Indir passes by, dressed in a new chadar. A child notices the new look and she explains that Raju bought it for her. The girls in the picnic are doubtful if Ranu would join them But Ranu does come and the group is happy.

This scene of children's picnic is intercut with the adult interaction between Sarbojaya and Indir. Indir comes wearing the chadar, Sarbojaya notices it and questions her about it. Indir's explanation that Raju gave it to her is not acceptable to Sarbojaya. For Sarbojaya it is as an afront to Harihar's pride that Indir should ask for a chadar from an outsider, more so when Harihar had promised to buy one for her. Indir talks about her desires and this infuriates Sarbojaya since everyone in this family has been delaying satisfaction of desires under the pressure of hard times. The quarrel builds up, leading Sarbojaya to ask Indir to leave immediately, since she has harmed the prestige of the family. Sarbojaya has a fit of coughing and Indir wants to help, but Sarbojaya sends her away angrily.

The serious scene of adult conflict is followed by a little quarrel in the girls group at the picnic about who was responsible for bringing salt. Ranu settles it by getting it herself. Durga has taken charge of the preparations for making khichdi, but Ranu does the actual cooking, which is praised by Durga. Here, Durga calculates the number of days for Ranu's marriage, and also makes light of the possibility of her own marriage saying that it would never happen.

Indir waits hesitantly by the pond as a group of children run across without noticing her. She goes to Raju's house asking for shelter there. We hear Raju's voice and see Raju's daughter coming in through the door of the house as the father speaks. This is the second time that Indir has left the house. The tune of Indir's song is heard behind this entire scene.

In the picnic we see Durga's growth in terms of managing the group activity. She puts everyone to work, approves of Apu when he brings a lot of firewood, and talks to Ranu who is her real age mate about the days left for the marriage. Others are still young and she bosses over them.The duplex world of adults and children is portrayed in this segment. There are issues of responsible behaviour and of carrying out one's duties in both cases. In the adult world it results in a breakaway in the relationship, in the children's world, it is softened by Ranu's action. She takes up the role of a grown up person.

The adult quarrel is about holding on basic dignity in poverty by not stepping out to beg from outsiders for needs. As the quarrel pushes Indir out of the ancestral house, she gets accepted readily in Raju's household, we notice that Raju welcomes her by offering those very things that Sarbojaya would refuse, a place to keep her things, water to wash her feet and a low stool to sit. Like daughters elsewhere, Raju's daughter is also being trained in household skills.

The door of Raju's house is seen from the inside as Indir walks in. Indir is composed entirely in terms of the door, as Raju welcomes her. We see many doors of houses throughout the film. The door of Harihar's house is constantly used as people go in and out. Earlier on we have seen the heraldic lion on the entrance of Shejobou's house, and now we see the door of Raju's house, and this is the only detail of Raju's house seen. In a like manner we see the outside of a very strong door of Nilmoni's house only once. Apu knocks at it on the morning of Durga's death. The door of a house is the dividing line of the private family matters to be kept inside, and the outside where one's honour and prestige must be protected. Throughout the Trilogy the door is brought into composition for its value of separating the exterior and the interior. The visual qualities of the doors carry the meaning in the narrative.The Trilogy uses doors in the design of narration in crucial ways. In AS, a door will be slammed and bolted on her own husband by Aparna's mother when she finds that the bridegroom is unsuitable for her daughter. In PP, the selling of ceremonial brass utensils hurts Sarbojaya's sense of pride and it has to be done stealthily, hence she tries to close the door behind her, but the door is incapable of holding on.

This is equally true for other parts of the architectural details of the house like the room interior, window, courtyard, terrace and staircase.

Film is a study of man in environment. Hence, in good composition, the foreground characters are consciously related to a detail of the environment which would make the foreground action more expressive. In this sense composing a character in relation to an interior detail like a door, or staircase or courtyard helps making deep narrative statements.

Puja-Jatra

The drummers come on in full beat for the Puja festivities as the Durga idol is set up in decorative regalia. Durga is in a new sari as she runs out of the door followed by Apu in new clothes and a new shawl tied by a delighted Sarbojaya. Children run in freely through Shejobou's door to the courtyard which houses the village idol for getting the ceremonial sweets being distributed by Shejobou in her courtyard. Apu and Durga get their share of the sweets. The drummers play on.

At night, a jatra performance in the traditional folk theatre style with garish make up and costumes tells the story of the serpent king's daughter Sujata who had married a human being. The father and son Mahakal threaten to kill the husband. Sujata pleads for her husband's life but fails. Eventually, she asks the husband to fight with the Demon, and she herself ends up crossing swords with the father. Apu is very much involved in the play.

The Puja is a festive event celebrated by the village community according to norms.The details like the drummers and the jatra players had been planned and talked about by Baidya Muzumdar in his gossip with the school master. It is also an occasion for new clothes for every one. Sarbojaya had talked of annual change of clothes in the kitchen scene (PP1.3). She is naturally delighted at the new clothes for the children,and Indir would have also got her promised shawl from Harihar if she had been patient. Also, the goddess Durga in her new clothes and finery is now located in Shejobou's compound and the children of the village run in freely for the sweets being distributed by Shejobou. Recall the earlier occasion when Shejobou had strong reservations about giving any sweets to Durga.

This scene is also a relief after the tension between Sarbojaya and Indir. It is a privileged moment which is used to weave in the community and the family. The puja-jatra scenes are worked with Apu and Durga in central positions in the composition. The Jatra performance stages a story that involves a human being insisting on survival with dignity.The decorated Durga idol provides tinsel that Durga had managed to get and Apu had used it for his crown.

PP-1.8 Childrens' Discovery of the Train Intercut with Last Quarrel between Sarbojaya and Indir

The jatra music continues over Apu's mirror shot in which he is trying to put on a moustache. He has also made a crown for himself. Durga comes in and while admiring his look, immediately gets suspicious about how he found the tinsel for his crown. She looks at her box and knows. A fight ensues and mother separates them. She adjusts Apu's crown while she admonishes Durga that a grown up girl like her could still need a toy box. Durga is ordered to go out and look for the cow. She leaves grimacing at Apu. He follows her. The children go running across the fields. PP theme music comes on.

This little scene has elements of childish playfulness along with Sarbojaya's role as the protective and corrective mother. She puts Durga on a chore and ties Apu's crown. Apu has staked a claim on Durga's property in the child's world. Durga is treating this as pilfering, and punishes Apu for this. Even after the little scuffle, Apu follows her all the same. They venture out into the meadows far beyond their normal beat. An overhead cloud passes across as they move on to distant unknown territory. The PP theme music covers them.

Indir comes walking with the aid of a stick, and of course, clad in the chadar. Sarbojaya is at her meal. Indir says that she wants to spend the last days of her life in her house. Sarbojaya is also determined to decline all efforts at reconciliation. When Indir moves to the kitchen to take some water, she offers Sarbojaya a last friendly smile which is also rejected. Indir loses all hope. She drinks some water. She waters the plant with the leftover in her pot, casts a lingering last look at her verandah and moves out.

There is no conciliation possible for Sarbojaya as long as Indir is clad in the offensive chadar. Indir is far too senile even to bother about these norms of propriety. However, she too has a sense of personal dignity. When she is denied shelter in her own house, she does not go back to Raju's house, but decides to die in the bamboo grove, which is just behind and closest to her ancestral house.

The children are now in a meadow with telegraph poles. Durga reaches a pole, and listens to its hum and looks up at the wires. Apu follows. They move through a field of tall *kaans* grass, where Apu has a sense of being lost. He calls for Durga who appears and gives a piece of sugarcane to Apu to chew. Then they become aware of the sound of the train. Both run towards the train. Durga trips and falls. Apu just reaches the embankment as the train roars by.

We see Apu-Durga relationship in a joint adventure in going beyond the village limits past the fields and meadow and moving into unfamiliar territory of the telegraph poles, the bund with the tall kaans flowers and eventually the railway track.. The physical environment is new to Durga. She is discovering for herself the humming sound of the telegraph poles and the sensation of being surrounded by tall kaans flowers. Apu loses his sense of direction. Visually we see Apu walking in a confused manner.He checks with Durga and she too doesn't seem to know or to care. He follows her and ultimately he succeeds in watching the train. The train comes on as a dark speeding mass sweeping across the frame of the quiet countryside. Compositionally the monstrous mass of the bottom of the carriage sweeps across the frame and across Apu's face as he just about struggles up the embankment to reach the level of the rails. This relationship of the lethal train wheels and human face anticipates Apu's suicide bid under the train when grieving for Aparna in AS.

The children return home with the calf, the PP theme music comes on again at the end of the adventure. In the bamboo grove they notice Indir squatting hunched up. The children approach in a playful mood as Durga goes to Indir and tries to wake her up, but she topples over and her head hits the ground with a thud. Her empty pot tumbles down into the pond and floats. Indir's song comes on in her own voice and continues as the pallbearers take her body for cremation. Apu and Durga mourn silently on Indir's verandah. Harihar returns from ritual bath and passes Sarbojaya without a word. Sarbojaya stands all alone as the song ends on her.

Indir's song in her own voice praying to be taken across the river underlies all actions following her death. The children are shocked at the sight of the dead, and the loss of their beloved Indir auntie. The pot, usually full of water is now floating empty on water. The community performs a smart job carrying the body, no longer in the chadar but wrapped according to custom in coarse white cloth for a quick cremation.Harihar seems to understand all that has happened but keeps quiet.The sequence ends on Sarbojaya, standing all alone. She will perhaps carry the guilt all her life.

As a portrayal of the aged, Indir brings out the characteristics of the old people who move away from norms while they get impatient about demanding and meeting their needs. The younger providers would, however do it at their own convenience. Thus the old remain helpless in fulfilling even their simple desires.

If we think back on Indir's death, another spiral moves through the film. It starts from the disapproval of Sarbojaya to her complete rejection of old Indir denying her the last wish to spend the last days of her life in the house Indir regarded as her own. The first disapproval was over the child Durga developing wrong habits, the second, more serious, was the honour of Harihar in buying her a chadar and the last was the effort at reconciliation by Indir. She eventually dies in the bamboo grove next to the house.

PP-1.9 Harihar Leaves to Earn More Money

Life goes on. A bioscopewallah comes to the village. The children are waiting at a broken wall for a coin they need to get a view into the box. In the house, Harihar prepares to leave and collects a box and other bundles and his umbrella. He should be back within a week or so, he says. As he moves away, Sarbojaya bows her head in a short prayer. As he comes out in the open, Apu runs up and asks him for money to have a look into the box. He gets it and both children run up to the box. Harihar is happy that the children are enjoying the show as he leaves.

Indir's death underlines the need for Harihar to exert more in the role of the provider. He had mentioned about a client in Dashghora, may be he could improve the earning by going there and seeking more work. This scene contains two main references. It links with the earlier scene when the sweetseller came and the children did not get the money. Here they do get the money to enjoy the views of faraway places like the Taj in Agra, the temple in Madras and the port in Bombay. The last time Harihar sees Durga she is already looking into the box at visions of another world.

The connections of the village with the outside world are presented here in physical terms by the train and telegraph poles. We also see some outsiders coming to the village like the sweetseller, and the jatra players, and now the bioscopewalla with the views of Bombay and Madras and other distant places. The children get to the peeping box as Harihar leaves. The first large movement of the narration is completed here, when Harihar has to move temporarily for earning more. Despite severe pressures, there is hope of better days ahead when Harihar returns.

PATHER PANCHALI - PART 2

The family holds on when Harihar is away temporarily

PP 2 has three parts as follows
Sarbojaya and Durga hold on
The Happy letter
Durga dies before Harihar returns

Sarbojaya and Durga Hold on

There are three sub-sections in this part.
10. The disappointing letter,
11. Sarbojaya sells utensils and
12. Ranu's marriage.

PP-2.10 The disappointing letter

Sarbojaya is working on making food preserves. Durga offers to help. However, she is asked to buy some jaggery so that something sweet is made for Apu. Just then Apu runs in announcing a letter. She picks it up and letter is read by the husband's voice on the soundtrack saying how he could not get the expected assignment due to deaths in the client's family. He is moving on to other places in search of work and will return after some delay. Sarbojaya's face darkens as she moves from medium to close while the disappointing news sinks in. Worried and distracted, she sits on the steps of the verandah. Precisely then a baul mendicant appears at the door requesting for his customary alms. Noticing that mother is too distracted to attend to the mendicant,Durga saves the situation, visually covering mother as she gives a bowlful of grain to the mendicant.

The second movement portrays the family while Harihar is away. Sarbojaya is capable of holding on Actually she is working on food for future use, and is just about to spend a pice for buying jaggery to make a sweet Apu has been asking for.But her confidence shakes with the husband's disappointing letter.The scene uses another aspect of the traditional village life, the wandering baul mendicant. This house is expected to give some grain to baul singers of devotional songs, as a part of social responsibility. The condition is getting dire though Durga finds enough in the house to save the situation. As she pours the grain, visually she covers distracted Sarbojaya sitting on the step with the letter in her hands. Compositionally, the interior- exterior distinction defined by the door is used yet again.

PP2.11 Sarbojaya sells utensils

Sarbojaya has reached the end of her provisions for the duration of Harihar's absence. She is making every pice stretch. But that cannot go on any more. Her clothes are torn and while she mends some at night she takes a decision to sell some costly ornamental utensils and manage the food for the family. She takes out the utensils from a wicker box with great deliberation. The PP Theme music starts from the point where early next morning she goes out of the house with the utensils, trying to close the door behind her, which has loosened and can hardly hold on. She returns with grain and puts it in the storing pot. Theme music ends here.

Sarbojaya has to think of ways to survive. She sells the costly utensils. This wordless scene is eloquent with choice of visual details of the properties used and lights and gestures. The heavy pace of taking out the plate and pot in the night,the irony that the plate has the inscription 'Besh Thak' (Be Happy) on it, the quick wary steps while leaving the house early next morning also attempting to go out unnoticed, the inability of the door to hold on closed, and the Pather Panchali theme music suggests the pain involved in the decision. The costly utensils were certainly part of the provision for Durga's marriage, possibly received by Sarbojaya in her own marriage. The need for sheer survival now has started consuming the provision for a later ccasion. Emotional ties are attached to the gifts connected with wedding, and this would be the last thing one would part with. Sarbojaya's strength of character shines out explicit in her action following the disappointing letter. She suffers within herself, quiet and lonely. But outwardly, she acts with strength to provide for the children on her own resources. She would not borrow money.

This scene prepares for the contrast of plenitude in the next sequence of Ranu's marriage. The marriage sequence has scenes of plenty.In effect, the marriage sequence is placed between two scenes of acute scarcity in Sarbojaya's family.

PP-2.12 Ranu's marriage

The scenes of Ranu's marriage are done involving the members of Harihar's family. From the outside Apu watches the bandplayers as they play an Irish marching tune 'It's a long way to Tiperrary', and so does the old priest who will perform the rituals. The community involvement in the marriage ceremony begins with the preparations and continues all the way. All the village elders are there. The village women have joined in the kitchen, preparing for the feast as they help with cutting vegetables as Shejobou organizes various chores. We notice Sarbojaya in the group. Her face is grave, and we know the reason why. In a room inside the bridal make up is going on and Durga watches as Ranu's feet are formally decorated. Ranu and Durga exchange smiles. At the ritual we see Ranu, the hand of the groom, the old priest, and Durga.

As we move from the outside of the house to the inside, the band music it continues in the food preparation scene, but at the ritual ceremony changes to Shehnai in the background. The last shot is a pensive closeup on Durga as she watches the wedding rituals.

Ranu's marriage is a festive occasion for the entire village community of the same kind as Apu's birth and at the Puja days. The community gathers around to share the joy. This happy occasion of the marriage of the daughter of a well-to-do household brings several old people, the priest who knows no retirement, the guests who enjoy sitting around and the bandplayers who have to earn their living by working on these celebrations. The bandplayers have come to the village from a bigger town. All the women including Sarbojaya are helping in the kitchen. Sarbojaya does not wear any special jewellery unlike some other women. Likewise, Durga is in contrast with Ranu in her bridal attire. This difference does not come in the way of their friendship. However the difference exists and it affects their material lives. They had talked about this day in the khichdi making scene and here they exchange meaningful glances and smiles.

Also recall our earlier discussion about the contrast between Ranu's marriage in PP and Apu's marriage in AS.

Harihar Expected but the Storm Comes First

PP-2.13 Letter with the good news

In the next scene, Nilmoni's Wife discovers that there is hardly any grain in Sarbojaya's pot even for the next meal. She leaves a coin with Sarbojaya disregarding her protests. Sarbojaya breaks into tears but she picks up the money after a while. She has no choice in the situation.

Just when she has reached the end of her resources, we open with a happy news contained in Harihar's second letter. Apu runs in with the letter and starts reading it, and Sarbojaya takes it from his hand and reads. Harihar's offscreen voice is heard as she reads the letter. He has found work, made some money and is returning soon. Her face brightens into a smile which dissolves to the ripples on the surface of a pond.

Nilmoni's Wife has always been a friend in need. Sarbojaya has strained the utmost and her efforts are still falling short and there is no grain left in the house. Sarbojaya's helpless tears and Nilmoni's Wife's determined action shows the struggle for dignity even amongst the closest circle of social relations. When the friend knows, she just leaves the money, disregarding Sarbojaya's protests.

The contrast between the first and the second letter is remarkable. The first letter created a threat to the image of the household, whereas the second letter creates a moment of joy in the privacy of Sarbojaya's personal world. Apu's growth in reading skill is seen as he starts reading the letter 'Shreemati Sarbojaya Devi...'

The dance of the bugs on the surface of the pond. The happy tune comes on and continues over the next shots of the cat and the dog in playful interaction and the bird in the cage and Sarbojaya fanning herself in a relaxed way as she lies on the verandah moving on to Durga preparing for a ritual.

This dissolve leads into a celebration of this happy moment as a dance of insects on the surface of a pond in a free and happy movement. This segment of sheer audio-visual pleasure serves to preface the mood of expectation and assurance of happiness with the expected arrival of Harihar. The moment of joy is extended to the elements in nature, the insects, then to the cat and dog playfully engaged and back to her and finally to the beginning of the next movement involving Durga in an exuberance of youth. (Refer to the earlier detailed discussion in the Dance of the Bugs.)

Durga is in a mirror shot, as she applies Kajal and bindi. She performs a ritual puja to a sapling, praying for a good husband. There is thunder in the air. A leisurely Apu munches muri (puffed rice) as he returns from school, while elderly people hurry homewards sensing the imminent heavy rain. Sarbojaya gets up. In contrast the kids rush out to soak in rain. Durga hurries through the end of ritual. She runs out of the house, banging the door. The banged door and the thunder arouse Sarbojaya and she calls out for Durga. Apu runs home, throws his schoolbag in through the window and without coming inside the house, runs in search of Durga. Sarbojaya attends to a priority job before the imminent rain : to take off the washing from the clothesline.

In case of the first letter, Durga had covered mother's prestige. In case of this second letter, she is not aware of the joy, but she has grown and started a 'brat' a ritual observance for a good husband. Durga's growth as an adolescent can also be seen in her changed behaviour pattern. She is taking interest in grooming her personal looks. She is also performing the ritual praying for a good husband. This makes a very different kind of sense coming after Ranu's marriage. Her lingering childhood and the upsurge of youth take her out in the open for enjoying the rain, Apu is an ally, not much involved in the joy of the adventure, but with her all the same.The difference in the reactions of children and adults to the imminent rain are interesting. Adults run in for shelter, children run out to be drenched.

The children run far away in the open field. A solitary Chakravarti fishing by the pond is surprised by a drop of rain falling on his bald head. He opens his umbrella as the rain picks up on the surface of the pond. Apu is drenched and shivering. He runs for shelter, the pet dog runs for shelter. Apu is shivering under a tree and calls out for Durga. Durga enjoys the full impact of rain on her face, on her body. When Apu calls she does not want to get away from the rain. She turns round and round, her hair soaking and swinging. Finally she runs and joins Apu trying to shelter him with her wet sari, recites a chant invoking the rain to stop. On the path by the pond, Sarbojaya is also out in the rain, with some edible vegetable leaves. She picks up a coconut, making sure that nobody sees her do so. Cut back to the children as Durga continues the chant and she sneezes. Background music accompanies the entire rain sequence.

Durga's lingering childhood merges with adolescent impulses as she enjoys the impact of rain on her body. Apu, still a child, prefers the safety of the shelter from the rain. Earlier we had reference to Durga's tendency to run a fever. Here, immediately after the wet exposure she sneezes, indicating her constitutional weakness, which develops into a serious illness. Apu who has also got wet in the heavy rain learns to be cautious.

We have seen so many variations of the behaviour of pilfering some trifle. Sarbojaya picks up the stray coconut from the path stealthily. The fruit is from a tree that was once owned by her and was lost in settling a doubtful debt of an older kin. Indir pilfers chillies from Sarbojaya's kitchen to meet a personal need which cannot be met by another means. For Durga pilfering from Shejobou's orchard is very simply a smart act for the sheer thrill of the act and for Indir's approval. Ranu pilfers a sweet for Durga simply for making a friend happy.When Apu took the tinsel from Durga's toybox for his crown, he was by right sharing what Durga had pilfered from the leftovers of ceremonial decorations of the Goddess Durga. And now, Sarbojaya pilfers.

PP-2.14 Durga dies before Harihar returns

The next scene starts with a village doctor examining Durga, as the worried Nilmoni, Nilmoni's Wife and Sarbojaya look on. The doctor alleviates adult anxiety by assuring that there is no need to worry. He advises light diet like sago, and cold pack on forehead if the fever rises. Nilmoni's Wife offers sago from her kitchen stock. Next, Apu is by Durga's bedside as they plan a future outing for a more relaxed view of the train. Next shot, through a window, the sweetseller passes by in the distance, but Durga's face is turned away, her eyes glazed in high fever. The PP theme music is heard in the background.

The moment of joy was shortlived. For Durga the fever has gripped her and she gets weaker, to the extent that she has no energy even to notice the sweetseller as he passes by. However, the desire to go and see the train again is still alive. The family has its severely depleted condition to deal with, and an illness adds to the lonely suffering of Sarbojaya.

From this illness, on to the stormy night when Durga dies. Sarbojaya sits by Durga's bed applying wet cloth to her forehead. Apu is fast asleep. The wind rises with flashes of lightning. The Ganapati idol is seen in the lightning flashes. The decrepit door rattles in the strong wind. Sarbojaya pulls a heavy trunk to prevent the door from breaking open. Durga tosses and turns in her bed. The window curtain breaks in the strong wind. Sarbojaya ties the curtain as Durga calls for her. Sarbojaya goes near the bed and places her head cheek to cheek protectively, trying to comfort Durga.The Ganapati image shakes violently in the flashes of lightning. Fade out.

Fade in next morning to Apu knocking the door of Nilmoni's house. Nilmoni's Wife comes in with Apu to the devastation of the courtyard and the collapsed roof of the kitchen hut. She moves in and sees Sarbojaya with Durga's head on her lap. She understands, as she touches Durga's wrist and sends Apu to call Nilmoni. She takes Sarbojaya in her arms trying to comfort her.

The events of Durga's illness and death are composed in terms of Sarbojaya's efforts to hold on and see things through till Harihar returns. She is numbed by the sheer effort of facing the devastation of that stormy night. The collapse of the kitchen roof is the working out of Sarbojaya's worst fears which she had been talking about for well over five years now. The event of Durga's death has been composed in the film as a young daughter's entreaty to her mother for protection and the mother's sheer inability even to comprehend, much less handle, any of the forces working actively on Durga. And who has understood, even among the wisest, the ever triumphing mechanics of Death ? Apu sleeps through the night just as Durga slept through the night of Apu's birth. Birth and death are adult matters. They do not touch children's world.

In retrospect, the other death in the film, Indir's, has also been narrated with details. Indir desired to spend the last days of her life in her ancestral home. When this was denied by Sarbojaya, Indir does not go back to Raju's house, or seek any other route to survival. She simply moves into the space nearest to the house the bamboo grove, sits there and dies. The circumstance is created by both the characters; Indir coming back with her last desire and Sarbojaya staying firm in her resolve. In case of Durga's death, the circumstances are created by natural forces which are beyond anybody's control.

The dead frog in the courtyard slush reminds us of the range of frog sounds we had heard at the night of Apu's birth. We have seen live animals linked with human action at the overtonal levels. Here we link the deaths, the human and the animal.

Indir's body is seen being carried across for the funeral. The last we see of Durga she seems to be lying quietly in her mother's lap. Later, we will be close to Harihar's dying moments and also, later to Sarbojaya's terminal hallucination. Aparna's death is much too tragic to be on screen: it is just reported in the narration.

Low and slow, Apu cleans his teeth all by himself with a faraway look in his eyes. Background music continues on actions. Sarbojaya draws water from the well in Shejobou's compound. Apu comes in after his bath, carefully crossing the slush in the courtyard. He combs his hair all by himself. He comes out of the room properly wrapped in his shawl carrying a bottle, perhaps to buy some oil. Halfway across the courtyard he looks up at the overcast sky, goes back inside the room and comes out with an umbrella under the arm. The background music ends here.

Death strikes here but life goes on. Sarbojaya and Apu continue their morning routines. Sarbojaya is lost in her deep grief. The day may be happy or tragic, fresh water from the well has to be drawn for the household needs. Apu has suddenly grown up after this experience.

Sarbojaya, even though lost within herself, has to cook food in Indir's verandah, now that her kitchen is in shambles. Nilmoni's daughter Bini comes in with vegetables sent by her mother. Sarbojaya is utterly unresponsive, which scares young Bini. As she turns to go, we notice her hair have been done in the four braid pattern that Durga had always wanted for her hair.

Harihar arrives. Sarbojaya hears him calling Apu and Durga. She responds by getting alert. Harihar is on the outside path, halts, as he takes in the devastation of the kitchen hut and he moves out of the frame while the camera keeps on looking at the kitchen area where one pot is still hanging bravely. Offscreen we hear the sound of the door as he enters the house, and then he comes in the courtyard beyond the kitchen space, calls out again for the children. Sarbojaya avoids facing him. She brings out his seat and his sandals and gives him water to wash his feet, and she turns to move away. Harihar stops her and starts showing the gifts he has brought with him. He starts with the kitchen rolling board, and the framed picture of the goddess Lakshmi. Next when he shows the sari he has brought for Durga, Sarbojaya breaks down. She collapses weeping but her cry is replaced by a piece of music which has been named as Mother's Wail. It takes Harihar some time to comprehend what had happened, and he too cries aloud, and collapses in physical contact with Sarbojaya. Mother's Wail also covers Apu coming home, as he halts, as if hesitating to get into the house.

While Harihar was away, Sarbojaya had withheld her grief. It breaks out with Durga's sari. The musical piece, Mother's Wail, carries all the pathos of her anguish. Harihar shares his grief by a physical contact with Sarbojaya.This is the only scene in PP where they touch each other. Harihar and Sarbojaya are together in the suffering, Apu who has shown signs of sudden maturity stops before entering the house.

At night, Sarbojaya and Apu are asleep, but Harihar lies wide awake. The whistle of a distant train is heard on his face. This is the point when he seems to come to a decision

The train whistle comes on his face as he lies awake in the night. This composition,the train whistle on the face at a moment of decision is repeated in moments of decision in APJT and AS as well.

PATHER PANCHALI - PART 3

PP-3.15 Harihar abandons the village home

The family is packing. Harihar handles some manuscripts. He calls Apu and asks him to clear the shelves. Sarbojaya is also packing and Nilmoni's Wife helps.They are talking of the conditions under which they are leaving. Shejobou comes in. She has brought with her a basket of fruit as a gift. Shejobou talks about the need for change.In the courtyard, the village elders arrive and sit around and ask Harihar about the propriety of his decision to leave his ancestral house. Harihar points out the impossibility of holding on.

Inside, as Apu reaches up the shelf, a coconut shell falls and with it the stolen necklace. A spider also creeps out. Apu picks up the stolen necklace. Background music of drums comes on. He jumps across the window to the side of the nearby pond and throws in the necklace.

Very early in the morning, the decimated family is moving away in a bullock cart. The pet dog has been left behind. A snake creeps out of the rubble, on to the verandah and crosses into the room. The bullock cart rolls on with the PP theme tune in the background, Sarbojaya breaks down in soft crying. Harihar and Apu are sad but composed.

In this segment events move very fast. Harihar, who was hoping to live on in his ancestral village, decides to leave. This again is done in three parts. The first part shows the parting and bidding farewell to the members of the community. The second part is a personal farewell for Apu as he discovers the stolen necklace and decides to maintain the dead sister's secret, the third, actual departure from the house itself. The village elders come in for a parting call, and making a formal plea that they were expecting that Harihar would consult the community seniors about making such an important decision like abandoning the ancestral house. Harihar is forthright as he explains how his struggles over fifteen years have been entirely frustrating. He wanted to write, he wanted the son to be educated, he wanted the daughter to grow, and none of these things have happened. For survival with dignity he must leave and go to Benares in the hope of a better life there.

Sarbojaya and Nilmoni's Wife continue to share their feelings of mutual amity and a sense of loss in the parting. Shejobou comes with a basket of fruit, offering it for their travel. This reminds us of Durga and her antics for pilfering fruit. Shejobou says that she too feels stagnated in the village. Staying at the same place for a long time makes one small minded. She also needs a change. These are thematically significant as psychological preparations for getting mobile, or leaving one's traditional abode. The triangles created in the opening scenes are resolved here as the three women converse amiably and by the gift of the fruit.

Apu's discovery of the necklace and his reactions reveal many things about him. He had grown up shared many things with Durga, but there were secrets also. Here was reminder of the violence she had faced. The drum music during Mother throwing Durga out of the house is now played on Apu as he picks up the necklace, jumps through the window, and ensures that no one sees him throw the necklace in the pond, watching the surface of the pond as the moss rearranges.The moss leaves an irregular circular pattern on the surface of the pond, similar to the hole in Indir's chadar. His question to her that night has been answered. But her secret must remain a secret.This is an important point in Apu's moral growth and development of his own sense of dignity.

The lived-in house is now deserted. The dog is left behind. A snake comes out of the rubble, wriggles up the verandah into the room where we had seen human beings move around. The snake has cultural overtones like the belief that snakes guard dwellings. The decimated family is in a bullock cart early in the morning. A lantern hangs below the bullock cart. Sarbojaya breaks down.Harihar makes no effort to help her. He know this will pass. The PP Theme tune covers the scene as the film fades out to the end.

The fiction of Nischindipur is placed during 1910-20 within a traditional village society in Bengal undergoing change under a complex of factors. In the extreme background are the new systems of administration, the railways and post office brought in by the British Raj. In the foreground story the family of Harihar Ray runs through its period of difficulties. The problem of food, clothing and shelter are woven into the routine of daily living but above all is the issue of surviving with dignity. Ultimately they have to abandon the ancestral village and migrate to Benares in search of a better living.

APARAJITO

Title and Title Music

The titles of APJT are written in the calligraphic style of printed book type.

In APJT, Apu's school and college education is at the printed book level, which is different from the manuscript style of PP. We have already noted that the visual style of the calligraphy of titles forms a design itself.

Also the Title Music (1) has the Apu Theme played on sitar, flute and sundari, composed in Bhatiali, a morning rag with an earthy feeling. It repeats at several points in the film with some variations.

The film has three divisions as follows:

APJT 1. Harihar starts a new pattern of life in Benares, which is strained by his illness and collapses at his death. Sarbojaya's effort to hold on fails. She leaves Benares for Manasapota, her uncle Bhabataran's village.

APJT 2. At Manasapota, Apu performs daily pujas as a Brahmin priest and in the day goes to school. He does well at studies. Six years pass. Apu is placed high at matriculation examination, and with encouragement from the Headmaster decides to go to Calcutta. However, he has to put up a short bitter stuggle with Sarbojaya to sort-of force her permission Eventually he goes to Calcutta.

APJT 3. In Calcutta Apu is drawn in by studies and pressure of living and the distance between Sarbojaya and Apu keeps on increasing. Eventually the lonely Sarbojaya dies. With the last link broken, Apu decides to give up the family profession and goes back to Calcutta for further studies.

APARAJITO – PART- 1

PATTERN OF LIVING IN BENARES

The year is 1920. Along with title music we hear the sound of a train made by the girders of the bridge. The view of the river front of Benares is seen from an incoming train on the Ganga bridge. (For the shape of the title music, see Index on Music.)

This incoming train begins the Benares phase for Apu's family. After a few months when the severely depleted family leaves Benares, the river front will be viewed on the Ganga bridge from on an outgoing train.

APJT PART 1 -A : Harihar's Moorings

1-A-(i) River Front Environment

The Benares ghats are seen at pre-dawn. A mendicant calls out the pigeons to feed them. The birds are all around, encircling the sky, crowding on ledges of platforms, sitting on the ghat umbrellas. Some pigeons come and cluster on a platform as the sun rises across the river on a lone widow seated in meditation.

Bunches of people, old and young, men, women, women with children on the river steps bathing, cleansing, some performing rituals. Harihar emerges having finished his bath, fills his spouted pot with the sacred water. The ghat keeper gives Harihar his spectacles deposited for security while he was bathing, and also vermillion for sacred tilak. He climbs slowly up the steps. As he moves, he offers the sacred water to wayside deities. He then goes into several narrow lanes leading to his house with a folksy village tune in the background.

This is a Hindi speaking area, but Bengali is understood and often used by Hindi speakers in talking to Bengalis

All the three films of the Trilogy

open with morning sequences. Morning to Day to Evening is a convenient script device for following the pattern of living of a character. It is also a logical device for a simple narrative while it has flexibility of emphasizing details of any activity of the character.

A morning dip in the sacred Ganga is a high religious priority in Benares. Harihar is now adjusting to a vastly different environment of Benares, certainly missing the village. His interaction with the ghat keeper recurs in the later scene when he faints. At that point after the bath Harihar forgets to take his spectacles and the ghatkeeper has to remind him.

Harihar is constantly relating himself to the wayside sacred icons. In the same manner he greets everyone who crosses him in the lane. The physical environment like the turns in the narrow lanes created by the brick walls of the houses is in severe contrast with the small winding path past the pool lined with the greenery of Nischindipur.

1-A-(ii) Family and neighbours

Harihar enters the door of his house, while Sarbojaya is busy around a running water tap in the tiny courtyard. She complains about Apu who, like a monkey, has run out without drinking milk to play with the unruly boys out there. There is no school nearby where Apu could study. She grumbles at the inconvenient crowding around her.

PP had begun with a morning scene in which Durga fed animals, the kitten. APJT begins with the feeding of pigeons. Sarbojaya's morning task was to fetch water for household needs from the well in Shejobou's compound. The running tap is a modern convenience in the Benares house.The new environment inside the house has one severe inconvenience for Sarbojaya. She is bothered by the lack of privacy.The neighbours live upstairs. The house entrance door is common and they have to cross the courtyard to get to the staircase.

The Pandey family comes down going out for their ritual bath. Pandey's Wife, speaking Hindi invites Sarbojaya to join them. Sarbojaya politely declines with a nod of the head. Pandey speaking a mix of Hindi and broken Bengali explains that she has come only lately and she is not yet settled enough for the morning routine of the Ganga bath. Everything will be done by her in due time, including the evening Vishwanath *aarti*.

Harihar emerges from the room into the courtyard, ready to go out, he is pleased to be told that there is a bowl of milk for him as well. Sarbojaya suggests a marketing list which now even includes a luxury item like *pan masala*. Harihar is sure that he can also get the famous Benares *malai* cream on credit from a sweet seller to whom he is giving herbal medicines. Sarbojaya is, however, doubtful of the efficacy of Harihar's herbs.

Apu is with newly found playmates. They run around in the narrow lanes in a hide and seek chase, negotiating obstacles like a cow blocking the lane. The background music in this scene is a variation of the Apu theme played on sitar and flute. Apu dashes into the house for a swig of water from the tap and is about to dash out when the mother detains him for his bowl of milk. He drinks the milk in a hurry and dashes out again telling her of the sweets his friends have given him.

The upstairs neighbour Nandababu comes down. He has a friendly gift of a calendar for Harihar. However, Nandababu explains that the calendar which has all the festival dates marked in red. Sarbojaya carefully avoids facing him. Nandababu goes in her room and fixes the calendar on the wall behind the bed.

In the design of social dynamics the firm norm bound village society generated strong triangularities. Here, the links are newly created and the sharp corners have not yet developed. Initially, the neighbours in Benares are strangers. They make Harihar's family comfortable in the new surroundings by common courtesies. However, they are not bound by any norms of social belonging, as happened in the village society. Hence, the social environment here has a mix of the benign Pandey and the potentially threatening Nandababu. The calendar gifted by him will be seen in all later scenes involving Harihar's illness. Apu's world is expanding. He has new friends to play with. One of them also gives him sweets.This reminds us of Ranu's gesture for Durga. Apu shouts out the names of the sweets he has eaten since the morning, which connects back to the list announced by Chinibas, the sweet seller, which Apu and Durga could not possibly buy. Harihar is clearly making more money. There is milk for both, Apu and himself.The promise of better life seems to be working out.

It is late morning. Apu wanders along the *ghats*. He observes Harihar in his professional routine as a *kathavachak* explaining the scriptures to an assembled group, mostly of women. Harihar has a sober and dignified style of presentation. Some distance away, on another *ghat*,

Kalicharan Bandopadhyaya presents mythological stories in a popular entertaining style designed to amuse his audience composed largely of widows. Apu also admires a body builder at his body building exercises. The wrestler is amused at Apu's interest and jokes with him inviting him to try out his exercises. Apu smilingly declines. Compositionally, Apu's head appears on the background of the ripples in the river.

The new environment gives Apu a chance to see his father at work reading the scriptures. Such observations and a possible comparison between Harihar and Kalicharan are never articulated by Apu. However, they are definitely a part of the experience which lead to his later decision against joining the priestly profession. Apu is also interested in observing the exercises of the body-builders. The coins in Harihar's collection dish are ready cash every day, a method of earning which is different from the uncertain mode of Nischindipur.

Snatches of singing, temple bells, recitations or instruments playing in a procession form the soundscape of Benares. There are several points when they are a part of the environment sound of a scene. The walls of the ghats have a liberal spread of handwritten advertisements, notably for tea. In the 1920s and thirtees, tea was being introduced as a beverage by careful marketing campaigns. The tea making and drinking scene around Sarbojaya, Harihar and Kalicharan Bandopadhyaya follows soon.

Apu's experiences in the new environment of Benaras include the hyper-strong muscles of the body-builder and later, of the immensely strong Vishwanath idol. The human face and feeling are quite often related visually to ripples and waves of water in many scenes in the Trilogy. Here Apu's face was related to ripples in the river, when he was interacting with the body builders. In PP Sarbojaya's smile on receiving the happy letter dissolves to ripples on the pond. In AS, the lost in grief after Aparna's death Apu on the seashore is related to the surge of the waves.

The evening sequence begins with very distant outdoor view of the flames of burning pyre on the cremation ghat. In her kitchen Sarbojaya pours kerosene in her stove to light it but her matchbox has only burnt out sticks. She covers her head as Nandababu comes home, crosses the courtyard and goes up the stairs. He has a cigarette dangling from his lips and he is carrying tabla drums. Sarbojaya avoids him by staying inside the kitchen. Then she goes across to the room and searches for matches. There are none, and Harihar is not in the house. She calls Apu, and as a last means sends him upstairs for borrowing from Nandababu the absolute minimum of just two matchsticks. Nandababu is settling down for a drink as Apu goes up two flights of stairs and asks for two matchsticks needed by his mother. Nandababu explains away the bottle by telling Apu that it is his medicine. Nandababu brushes aside the very idea of two match sticks only. Instead, he insists on sending a whole matchbox for Sarbojaya with the message that she need not return it.

Apu experiences the dark secretive routine of Nandababu hastily explains away the liquor bottle as his medicine. Also, sending a whole matchbox with the message that Sarbojaya need not return it could be a misreading of the request for matchsticks as a silent message from her. This could have made Nandababu bold enough to attempt his advance to her later.

Another day, at the end of his *katha* Harihar is greeted by Kalicharan Bandopadhyay. He has been carrying around a packet of tea leaves. As a bachelor he has no place to get the tea brewed. Harihar invites him to his house and Sarbojaya prepares tea for the first time in this household. She is pleased at the praise from the guest. Kalicharan admires Apu and offers to take him along for a forthcoming formal feast. Kalicharan talks of the need for a family and confides to Harihar that he has been saving money for his plan to get married. He asks Harihar if he knew of any woman he could marry. As Kalicharan does the parting greetings in the lane, we hear offscreen sounds of playing of the *tabla*.

Another day, another man in the house. This is a new situation for Sarbojaya. Kalicharan reacts to the benign presence of a woman of the family at the source of happiness for Harihar. Upstairs, Nandababu at the tabla presents the erotic attitude. The scene connects three men in a triangle around Sarbojaya's womanliness.

The new pattern of life at Benares differs vastly from the village mode of PP. The physical environment of stone ghats and buildings here are distinct from the soft brick and earthen structures of Nishchindipur. In Benares it is a congested riverside contrasted with the shrubs, trees and ponds of Nishchindipur. Some walls in the lanes are decorated with paintings of animals, dog, cow, even the regal elephant, horse, and camel as if trying to lift the dreary status of these lowly lanes and dwellings. In the village one accosts real animals – cow, dog, cat, geese and frogs. Also the city lanes are quite unlike the paths in the village. The greenery of the village is missing here. However, the ever present Ganga and the ghats, the steep steps and the narrow lanes have an overbearing presence. They provide the physical frame within which the children's world is shaped differently from the adult world. The adults move around the river, the shrines, and dwellings. The children create their play and exploration in the narrow lanes. Harihar's dwelling here is very different from the village house. The upstairs neighbours also use the main door of the building and the courtyard, causing inconvenient lack of privacy for Sarbojaya. Harihar does talk of moving to a better house later which would also be convenient for Apu's schooling. Apu has not yet joined any school, but he is learning all the time.

1-A–(iii) Prayers to the Presiding Deity

The Vishwanath Temple golden spires point skywards while two pigeons settle down on a ledge. Heavy crowds move in and out through the ornate gates. Sarbojaya and Apu go inside the temple for the evening arati. The collective chanting of the priests is accompanied by heavy sounds of big cymbals and big drums. Sarbojaya and Apu are drawn in by the sheer weight of the ornate spectacle and heavy sounds. Outside, the Dussehra celebration fireworks are on.

Benares has a routine of organized religious activity. The presiding deity is Vishwanath. The evening Arati is the daily ritual attracting a wide range of worshippers. For Sarbojaya, it is the mere observance of a religious duty. Apu watches the elaborate spectacle with the same kind of interest as he would for the jatra or the band players in the village or the body builder on the ghats. The experience of the awesome deity and the immensely involved crowd present at the elaborate ritual is widely different from the individuated simplicity of lighting a lamp and blowing a conch for the evening worship in Nischindipur.

Part 1– B: Stress on Pattern of Living

1-B –(i) Harihar is ill

Sarbojaya is lighting the festive lamps as Harihar enters the door. As she asks if he would take Apu to the Ramleela, she realises that he is unwell. He had felt faint after the evening prayers when climbing up the steep steps of the ghats. Sarbojaya suggests consulting a doctor but Harihar would rather use his own herbal medicine. Sarbojaya is skeptical; nevertheless she follows Harihar's instructions and administers the medicine. Apu comes in with a sparkler. Apu sits with his father and they talk of comparing the variety of fireworks here with those of the village. One of Apu's friends, Shambhu has been teaching him English. Harihar is happy when he confirms that Apu can translate confidently the relevant Bengali sentence into "Apu is a good boy". Apu goes out as Shambhu calls him for lighting the fireworks. Harihar assures Sarbojaya that his medicine is working and he already feels better. Harihar continues to talk of more cheerful things like shifting soon to an affordable, better ventilated two-roomed house, close to a school and market. They watch Apu humming a tune as he works on making some plaything.

This scene evokes many threads that would be worked out later. Sarbojaya is skeptical about Harihar's medicine. Interestingly, she uses Harihar's leftover stock of herbal medicines herself later in the village Manasapota when she feels unwell. Apu's expanding world is taking in the variety of fireworks, and also the English language. Harihar approves Apu's informal learning. He is planning to shift to a house that would be close to the two important places, the school for Apu, and the market for provisions needed for daily living.

The next morning a monkey at the tap frightens Sarbojaya. Also, Harihar is ready to go out for the ritual river bath making light of the illness last evening. Sarbojaya tries to dissuade him. He goes out, despite. However, after the bath Harihar is really unsteady. The *ghat* keeper points out that he has forgotten to pick up his spectacles. He falters while climbing up the steps. And then, he collapses on the steps in a faint. A flock of pigeon flies away as he falls People around rush to help and give physical support to move him along the lanes upto his house. The background music piece in Raag Marwa played on *sarod* accompanies the scene from the faint to the door of the house.

A doctor diagnoses chest congestion and prescribes massage and protective measures in the damp room. Pandey offers to go with the doctor and get the medicine. Nandababu watches and enquires from a distance. Sarbojaya holds on steady and well composed. Pandey's Wife, the good neighbour assures of every help which Sarbojaya could ask for without any hesitation.

After the last evening's illness, Sarbojaya makes the commonsense attempt to prevent Harihar from straining himself this morning by going out for the river bath. Harihar goes out all the same. He cannot manage climbing the ghat steps and faints. His head is composed against the river ripples in the background as he gradually loses consciousness. As he falls he is shown as a distant figure enclosed by the dark shadows of the buildings, as if seen from the point of view of a widow coming down the lane. The people nearby help him reach home.

The social interactions here look similar to those in the village, but with a qualitative difference. The neighbours are helpful, but distant. The Pandey couple reminds us of Nilmoni and his wife at the time of Durga's illness.. But the intimacy of Nilmoni's Wife is missing. Nanda babu is present, but distant like Shejobou at the time of Apu's birth. Here we notice similar pattern in the two neighbours. The doctor here is more sophisticated than the doctor who had come in for Durga's illness.

1- B- (ii) Tension increases. Harihar dies

Apu is out of the house moving around in the streets watching interesting things like bullocks drawing a leather bucket full of water from a well. At home, Nandababu comes down the stairs, pushing aside a kitten which is in the way. First he calls out softly for Harihar and ensures that he is not awake. Sarbojaya has heard Nandababu and feels alarmed. Then he moves stealthily towards Sarbojaya in the kitchen. He removes his shoes and steps in to test an amorous advance by asking if "sister-in-law" was preparing a betel leaf *paan* for him. Sarbojaya reacts ferociously. She brandishes a curved kitchen knife and hisses at the lecherous man to clear out. Nandababu withdraws and moves away instantly. Sarbojaya gasps in sheer exhaustion. Dissolve to the loud ritual of the Vishwanath Aarati. Late night, Sarbojaya massages Harihar's chest while her disturbed face seems lost in worry over Harihar's health and the danger sensed in the unsavoury event of the day.

Nandababu's advance triggers off Sarbojaya to assert her dignity fully. The sheer force of her reaction pushes back Nandababu. In visual composition Sarbojaya wields the kitchen knife in frontal view with Nandababu's bulky back in camera foreground.This is the point of climax in the portrayal of Sarbojaya's strength of character. She was a strong mother so far, caring for the reputation of children and a good wife, caring for her husband's reputation. Here she defends her own chastity as a strong woman. In the urban context of Benaras, norms are slackened and a woman has to fend for herself. Nandababu had taken a calculated step. Sarbojaya's response was immediate.

The sudden activation of a woman's potential strength is seen again in AS when Aparna's Mother pushes her own husband unceremoniously out of the room, shuts and bars the door against him to ensure protection to the daughter from an imminent unsuitable marriage..

There is a rising spiral of Sarbojaya's fears now. It started this morning with the monkey challenging her right to the water tap. Then shortly after Harihar insists on going for the river bath despite the illness last evening. And sure enough Harihar is brought back home in a faint, from which he hardly ever recovers. And then, Nandababu. He assures that Harihar is in coma before he ventures this ugly threat to her very sanctity as a wife. This is the top of the spiral fear. It has no possible relief since she cannot share it with anyone. She has to suffer it within herself, alone. The second arti looks like a desperate prayer for help from the presiding deity. When Harihar is around she has an inbuilt ambient protection. In the late night shot when she sits up massaging Harihar's chest, her face clearly show this quality of fear. The next movement will lead to Harihar's death and the breakdown of the Benares pattern of life.

The city is silent in the pre-dawn hour. Harihar wakes up suddenly, gasping with weird sounds and asks for *Ganga* water. Sarbojaya is alarmed. She searches but there is no sacred water in the house. She wakes up Apu and sends him to get a potful from the river. Apu is not aware of the imminent crisis as he moves through the lanes and down the steps to the river bank. He even slows down to admire a bodybuilder at exercise. Sarbojaya helps Apu pour the holy Ganga water in Harihar's mouth as his eyes bulge out at the moment of death. Sarbojaya lets out a sharp exclamatory cry, "Ki Holo?" (what's happened?) A flock of riverside pigeons suddenly fly off and circle twice in the early dawn sky. Next, the tenth day mourning as Apu is formally clothed for the purification shradha. He is led by some elders along the river bank. Music passage in rag Jog underlines the Death sequence (For detail see Music Appendix).

Harihar's Death Music is repeated in APJT and AS in situations which have similar quality of helplessness.

When his father dies in Benares, Apu is too young to comprehend the details as he is guided through the tenth day shradha rites by elderly neighbours. Several years later after Sarbojaya's death in Manasapota, the older, more determined Apu returns to Calcutta immediately for studies without staying in the village for the stipulated days for shradha. He says he would take care of all that at Kalighat.

The new pattern of living in Benares is cut off even before Harihar had settled down. In the changed situation, Sarbojaya will have to provide for herself and Apu, and also ensure his growth in a dignified manner.

1-B - (iii) Sarbojaya tries to hold on

Sarbojaya has by now taken up the job of a cook in a rich household in Benares. Bhabataran, an uncle of Sarbojaya, is a priest based in village Manasapota in Bengal. However, the old man desires to live in Benares in the last years of his life. At present he is here on the annual pilgrimage and comes to meet Sarbojaya. He suggests the alternative that she could go back to Bengal and live with Apu at Manasapota in Bhabataran's house. Apu has been listening and does not seem to be happy. Sarbojaya asks for sometime to think it over.

Sarbojaya takes up the only job she could possibly do, a cook in a rich household.This arrangement takes care of the immediate needs of survival and security, and of education for Apu. Uncle Bhabataran's offer implies that the ten year old Apu is grown up enough to replace the old man as the resident Brahmin priest of the teli (oil trader) family in Manasapota. This regular professional job for Apu would ensure a comfortable life for Sarbojaya. The Benares job implies that Apu would have the status of a cook's son, being ordered around for odd jobs, which is an unhappy prospect.

The master of the house dozes in an armchair, while Apu is plucking out grey hair from his thinning head. He wakes up with a start, the job ends, and Apu is tipped a coin with disdain and dismissed. Apu immediately runs out of the house and uses the coin for buying peanuts. He goes inside a temple with a marble verandah and ornately carved pillars. The place is full of monkeys. Apu calls out to the monkeys and enjoys himself feeding them peanuts.

1-C Sarbojaya abandons Benares

The lady of the family tells Sarbojaya that they are due to leave Benares for their village next month. They like her cooking. Since she has has no relatives here or elsewhere, Sarbojaya could continue in this job and accompany them. She has yet to make up her mind. After meeting the lady, as Sarbojaya comes out of room down the stairs, she sees Apu in the verandah below. He is blowing the cinders in the chillum he is carrying for the master's hukkah. Such future prospect for Apu as a boy servant is simply not acceptable to the mother in Sarbojaya. Instantly, she decides to give up this job and go along uncle Bhabataran's suggestion. Her decision is instantaneous. An engine whistle sound comes right on Sarbojaya's face as she steps down the stairs and there is a swish pan to the train carrying Bhabataran, Sarbojaya and Apu moving on the bridge away from the Benares from where the view of the ghat front recedes.

The Benares phase had started with a view of the river front from a train on the bridge approaching Benares. The Benares phase ends with the characters leaving the city on an outgoing train crossing the bridge in a symmetrically reverse shot showing the receding river front.

A distant train whistle on a face is a device used at several crucial moments in the narrative design of the Trilogy. The placing the whistle on the face is overtonally related to the purpose of the change triggered of. In PP the whistle is heard late at night on Harihar's serious face as he lies sleepless when deciding to abandon the village. In APJT, the whistle sound is placed on Sarbojaya's face as she moves down the staircase as she takes the instant decision to leave Benares. In AS, following Aparna's death, Apu has been lying in his room in dry eyed mourning and when he stirs to look at his tearless face in the mirror, the railway whistle comes on his reflection. He moves out to the railway siding, contemplating suicide. The compositional difference in placing the whistle on the face in the three films is expressed overtonally in the difference of quality of the event associated with the whistle in each case.

The train runs along the tiled villages of eastern UP, through the night across south Bihar. Next morning, as it enters the extensive fields and palm fringed landscape of Bengal, Sarbojaya has the mere trace of a smile on her face. The *Pather Panchali* theme tune provides background music in Bengal from the train to a bullock cart, to moving on foot along the pond to arrive at the house in Manasapota.

APARAJITO – PART 2

STRESSED PATTERN- MANASPOTA TO CALCUTTA

2 –A : Apu as student–cum-reluctant priest

As she enters her new house with solid mud walls, clean and complete, Sarbojaya simply sits down in a verandah overwhelmed, while Apu has moved to the back door. Looking beyond the fields, on the horizon is a rail track. Apu calls out for her and Sarbojaya joins Apu while looking at a distant passing train.

In the evening Nirupama, the widowed daughter of the patron's family brings firewood and enquires about food provisions, as Apu runs out to see the evening train. During the evening meal Bhabataran makes it clear that he would be going away after a week or so, hence Apu's training as a priest should start immediately. This was the tacit agreement between Bhabataran and the now-firmly-smiling Sarbojaya. Apu listens on doubtfully to the decision-making adults. He is too young to intervene in the matter.

Having tried and failed to survive with dignity in Benaras. Sarbojaya prefers living in the village in Bengal. This is closer to her frame of comfort since it also provides Apu a possible continuation of the father's profession.The relaxed rural environment at Manasapota, the pond and its go-along pathway is also quite like Nischindipur.The house is comfortable and self-contained, even has a well of its own. And, of course, everything here is a relief from the grind and always-on-the–edge feel of Benares life. Nirupama, the widowed daughter of the patron household takes to Sarbojaya with a daughter-like affection, helping her all along in many ways. The train is a regular presence here, every morning and evening. Apu is excited and delighted about it. Eventually the train would also take Apu away to Calcutta.

Bhabataran starts instructing Apu in the rituals of worship to be performed every morning in the patron's house. After Bhabataran leaves, Nirupama informally takes over and continues the training. One day, Apu, now a family priest returns from the patron's house carrying in a basket the idol on throne he had taken there for the morning worship. He sees boys of his age play around and fight and enjoy themselves. Apu hastens to reach home to leave the sacred basket there, and runs out again. He observes from a distance boys run towards the school as the bell calls them for their classes.

Apu lies pensively in bed at night. Sarbojaya senses his unhappiness. Is he missing Benares or Nischindipur ? or, is he not happy with the work? She goes on to explain her vision of the future. If Apu is good at his priestly duties the rich patron will also care well for both of them. In due time they may even be able to return to Nischindipur. Apu cuts her short at this point suddenly asking if he can go to school. Sarbojaya's initial objections are easily met. His work as a priest involves only the morning. During the day he could go to school. When Sarbojaya raises the question who would pay for studies, Apu asks the counterquestion which would touch any adult heart :"Don't you have any money put away, mother?" That settles the issue. Sarbojaya thinks for a moment. If going to school would make Apu happy, Sarbojaya would certainly spend the money. Sure enough she has money and Apu would certainly go to school.

His daily morning duty would be to go to the patron's house to perform the puja of an idol, which, by convention, can be touched only by a Brahmin. Apu has been pushed into professional priesthood work. However, he has not ceased to be a young boy. He sees the playing boys around him, who also go to school in a nearby locality. He wants to be like them. The school beckons him.

This small scene between Sarbojaya and Apu has several earlier references. Apu was at school in Nischindipur. Harihar and Sarbojaya both wanted Apu to be sent to school in Benares, though it could not quite work out there. Apu had playmates who went to English teaching schools. Harihar had even commended Apu for learning English from a friend, even though it was one sentence. However, Harihar died all too suddenly, and now Sarbojaya prefers the safe choice of the traditional family profession for Apu. In Manasapota, with the young Apu already engaged as a priest in the rich patron's house, she can dream of returning to Nischindipur later with a fully trained adult son. She could then repair their house, reclaim lost privileges and really settle down. Sarbojaya's sensitive questioning about the cause of his unhappiness triggers off Apu to ask if he could go to school. The protective mother will

have to spend money if school-going would make Apu happy. However, she expects that Apu would continue to be in the family profession even after he has been through school. Here is the source of the distancing between Apu and Sarbojaya, basically in her ignorance of the process of education. She could never foresee that education will open up Apu's mind to the modern world of knowledge and lead him away from beliefs around traditional life style of a priest. She is hardly aware that her own norms of respectable livelihood will face severe challenge when Apu gets increasingly involved with the wider modern knowledge.

The school building and compound are all spruced up to welcome the Inspector, who is due in just half an hour. The Headmaster is all tensed up and checks minor corrective jobs like some stray paper on the floor which has to be removed, or a scribbled caricature of him on the wall, wiped clean and a stray cow chased away from the school compound. The Inspector arrives in a horse drawn buggey with a peon in attendance. During the class inspection, the Inspector is deeply moved by Apu's effective recitation of a patriotic poem celebrating the beauties of Bengal. A snatch of the *Pather Panchali* theme tune is heard towards

the end of the recitation.

The school itself functions within the framework set up by the administration for the modern educational system to reach the middle levels of rural society in Bengal. This formal quality can be seen all the time, even in the standard L shaped symmetry of the building,which is located on a kaccha village road suitable for horse driven carriages. The Inspector from the headquarters is formally dressed in a three piece suit with tie, buttonhole flower, closed shoes and sola hat. A stray cow which had been driven out of the compound however gets into the way and is sort of touched aside by the Inspector as he walks on the pathway to the school.

The school has much discipline, but also flexibility of personal attention to bright individual students. The Headmaster is also delighted with Apu's performance. He encourages Apu with sound advice on ambition to know of the wide world out there even though they are located in a backward rural area of Bengal. He gives him books to read on varied subjects, on geography, on travels and discoveries and stories of inventions and biographies of scientists like Galileo, Archimedes, Newton, Faraday.

Apu lives by the knowledge he is

acquiring from the books. He uses household pots to device a siphon system. He attempts explaining to mother the process of lunar eclipse using a lantern as Sun and two round fruits as the Earth and the Moon. On another occasion, he dresses up and dances like an Zulu tribal shouting "Africa", "Africa" startling the mother. Studying by kerosene lantern at night, he drops off to sleep, spilling ink on the notebook. Sarbojaya has to shake him awake for meals. Time goes on – fade out.

Apu's mind has started opening up. His innovative toys involve practical application of scientific principles. He tries out a tribal dance as if it is a practical exercise for imbibing the knowledge of travel and discovery. It reminds of Apu dressing as a prince with a moustache and crown in Pather Panchali after the jatra play. It also anticipates Apu's son Kajal moving around with a mask when he is introduced as a young boy in Apur Sansar. Sarbojaya's lack of comprehension of what Apu is learning and talking about becomes another aspect of the distancing between them. Falling off asleep while writing anticipates the opening scene of AS when Apu gets up in the morning, having gone to sleep while writing his novel, and this lack of care has spilt ink on the bed linen.

2–B – Apu forces Sarbojaya to agree for Calcutta studies

Six years have passed. The Headmaster tells Apu, now an awkward sixteen-year old, of his second rank in the district at the matriculation examination. This carries a scholarship of ten rupees per month for further studies. Apu would certainly like to continue study science and the Headmaster would also help find a place for him for lodging in Calcutta. However, the mother's willingness is a crucial element in the situation. Apu says he will need to persuade her to agree.

The Headmaster interacting with Apu is compositionally similar to and anticipates the opening of AS where a college professor admires Apu's skill as a writer when giving a personal certificate to him.

Sarbojaya is grinding some herbal medicine, which she quickly licks and hides away as she hears Apu come in the house. The herbs are certainly from Harihar's leftover stock. Sarbojaya was then doubtful of their efficacy, but she is using them now. Apu comes with a globe given to him by the Headmaster. Sarbojaya is delighted when he explains his high position in the examination result and the considerable sum of ten rupees as scholarship to go with it. However, when she understands that to get the scholarship he will have to study further and go to Calcutta, the smile fades and she reacts against it. The sound of a train can be heard behind her anxious close up. Apu thinks he can divert her by showing her the globe asking if she knows what this is. Compositionally the shadow of the globe falls on her face. She frowns and moves away into the room, leaving Apu disheartened.

Apu follows her inside the room which has dim evening half lights. She is set against his going to Calcutta. He explains how the Headmaster is arranging for a place to stay. The scholarship money with half fees in college and some part time work will take care of expenses. Sarbojaya brandishes the bitter fact that when Apu leaves his job as a priest, it implies that Sarbojaya would be left without any support, since the patron family would not continue to support her when they are not receiving Apu's service.The argument about Apu's future prospects and her immediate needs turns sour when Apu derides the priestly profession itself. As the argument heats up, Sarbojaya slaps Apu. They separate, both hurt and angry. Then, with practical wisdom, Sarbojaya realises that Apu will have his way, and that she has no choice in the matter. She decides to agree with Apu and smoothen out the transition of his going to Calcutta. She brings out her money savings of thirty two rupee coins for use in the necessary preparations. Apu behaves as if he has won a big struggle. With great enthusiasm he tries to show her the location of Calcutta on his globe.

This is an interaction in which two mindsets confront each other and clash. Sarbojaya is all for the ancestral profession of priesthood which has ensured a simple life for their family over the generations. She also adds on her maternal authority as she orders Apu to continue this option. Apu is now a sixteen year adolescent mind which has been opened up by modern knowledge. He is all set out for further college education, and while in doing so he also derides the priestly profession and defies the mother outright. In an uncontrolled fit of anger, Sarbojaya slaps Apu. Of course, she makes up soon enough when she realises that Apu is determined to have his way. She gets set to make the best possible arrangements for Apu to go to Calcutta. He rejoices as if he has triumphed in a battle. He is utterly insensitive to the silent suffering inherent in the mother's decision. Compare the scene in PP when Durga is punished. In case of Durga, Sarbojaya had to face an insult because of Durga's bad reputation. Here the son was refusing to regard the family profession as worthwhile. Her anger in both cases is intense but controlled quickly with more rational reasoning.

The morning of departure begins with Sarbojaya packing for Apu. Some food provisions are packed in a tin trunk with Apu's personal things as also with two postcards for prompt writing of his safe journey to mother. And a bedroll with his clothes in it. The globe does not fit inside the trunk. It will have to be carried in Apu's hand all the time. He is given money, twenty five rupees from mother and a gift of five rupees from Nirupama.

As Apu leaves walking away on the poolside path, Sarbojaya stands at the door ready with a smiling face since she knows that he will turn his head back for a parting last look. A moment after this display the same face gets lost in infinite sadness.

During the railway journey, Apu continues to be deeply involved in the globe in his hand. From the railway station he walks along the crowded streets of Calcutta and seeks out the New Royal Press, where the owner, Akhil Babu is a friend of the Headmaster. Akhil Babu offers him free stay sharing his room. Apu could compensate by working the night shift in the press. The room has electric light, a new experience which Apu reports in the letter to his mother.

Leaving Manasapota, the train journey and arrival in Calcutta form the beginning of the new life to be faced by Apu. It is a sharp shift away from mother in physical as also psychological sense. Sarobjaya had no comprehension whatsoever of the various things Apu was learning at school. Yet, physically Apu continued his priestly duties, even while he was learning new things with modern education. Now, he will be away, she will no longer play her role as Apu's protector. Apu's life, however, is going to be vastly different from anything she can even imagine.

During the train journey, Apu remains absorbed in looking at the details on the globe and is oblivious of other passengers in the compartment. Even a hawker selling painkiller balm does not succeed in drawing his attention. The painkiller balm could well be a distant overtone of bottle labeling in a pharmaceutical factory in Calcutta where Apu would be looking for a job in AS. The train is a device that separates people. Here it is mother and son, in AS it will be husband and wife.

In Calcutta, Apu experiences for the first time city crowds, busy streets like Harrison Road, and new kinds of localities. In Patuatola Lane where the New Royal Press is located, a car passes by while children at a hand pump are enjoying themselves improvising a bath. It is all very different from the village. There is hardly any trace of the open greenery of Nature. When Apu reaches the room he will share with Akhil Babu the press owner, he is delighted to switch on and off an electric light for the first time in his life. This newcomer from a village will learn a lot while negotiating this new environment.

In APJT, the train gets placed within the big railway system. In PP it was just a distant whistle and a monstrous blur that crossed the tiny watchful face of Apu at the embankment. In APJT it is a routine, the massive engineering of the bridge and the system of the major railway station with its tracks and platforms, and the unrelated crowds that use the facility. All these get closer to Apu's life and his object of childhood fascination now simply becomes a facility for travelling.

2-C Apu-Sarbojaya strain increases

Apu is occupied in his college classes during the day and works part of the night in the press. This day Apu and college friend Shibnath have been turned out of the class by a teacher for being inattentive. As they recline on a riverside lawn with steamer traffic in the back, Shibnath talks of the ambition of going abroad. Apu is morose since his ambitions are being thwarted by his mother. He recalls with distinct bitterness his struggle with Sarbojaya who would have him there stuck as a priest in Manasapota, and would not let him move for college studies even in Calcutta which is only a few hours away from the village.

The social circle around Apu is very different from his experience so far. He develops new friendships in the college. Ambitions open up and begin formulating in his mind though in reality he is bound by his mother's ideas. He is not an angry young man but someone straining at the strong bonds that tie him to his past. His college friend Shibnath has his confidence now. Another friend Pulu will be a very important figure in his life in AS.

The teacher and the classroom in

the college are qualitatively more distant compared to the village school. Despite formalities, the school had a more human contact and appreciation of a student's individual situation. Apu's life as a day time student with part time work in the press is much harder than his life as a part time priest in the village.

APARAJITO – PART 3 THE BOND SNAPS

3-A-The first holiday is a strain on Apu

Sarbojaya sits alone under a tree as the evening train passes by in the distance. Apu is due to arrive home for a short holiday. Sarbojaya brings out a low stool and towel. She begins to draw water from the well, just when Apu is heard calling, she smiles and turns towards the door. The bucket falls back in the well with a splash, tugging at the rope which is tied to the branch of a tree. Apu arrives and after a short exchange with her about this and that, he rushes out for a dip in the pond. At the evening meal, Sarbojaya asks about his arrangement for food in Calcutta. Apu makes her happy by saying that her cooking is better than that of the cook in Calcutta. She prods him on to talk of the various places seen by him in Calcutta. Apu is reluctant to talk as he is sleepy. When he mentions,among other places, Kalighat and Keortala the burning ghat, we hear Harihar's death music strains in the background as Sarbojaya shifts to warn against crossing roads in a hurry in Calcutta. Then she keeps on telling him how she is dreaming of living with him when he settles down with a job. Her health is failing and she asks pointedly if Apu would attend to her illness in preference of his studies. She notices with dismay that Apu is not listening to her. He is fast asleep.

Apu's visit home is joy for Sarbojaya, also an opportunity to tell him about her concerns. She has been quiet about many things in her loneliness. Apu,in any case, is not sensitive to her needs and sleeps off even as she talks. She would certainly be reminded of a similar occasion in Nischindipur when Harihar slept off while she was telling him about her frustrated dreams. Way through from PP her cooking has been specially mentioned. Later, in APJT her Benares employers like her cooking skills. Reminder of death by the mention of burning ghat makes her uneasy and she tries to change the topic of conversation.

Next day Apu feels bored in the village. The visiting acrobat is below his level of interest. The main performer, a boy of his own age bends backwards holding his ankles and walks on rhythmically to his master's chant saying: "you show your super skills..." etc. Apu is not even interested in savouring a *paan* made for him by Sarbojaya, nor does he plan to call at Nirupama's house. While settling to sleep he consults the almanac asking mother to wake him up before sunrise well in time for the morning train. Sarbojaya hesitates to wake him up in the morning hoping that he would sleep on and stay another day. However, he does wake up with a start and irritably continues preparations to leave. He is at the railway station well in time, but when the train arrives he decides at the last moment against going away. He comes back home for another day with mother but promptly settles down to catch up sleep.

The relationship between mother and son is strained. Apu is bored in the village to the extent of cutting short his stay which involves leaving the mother as well when he has a strong urge to continue being with her. This silent wavering between the two mutually exclusive positions is a subtle aspect of Apu's adolescence. The mother's naive expectation that if he oversleeps he would stay another day is more intensely satisfied by Apu's return. His need to catch up with sleep lost in the night working duties in the printing press is an aspect of his condition that the mother does not know.

Apu's response to the acrobatic skill is very different from the childhood response to the Jatra performance. He was impressed then, in contrast, he is bored now. Excellence of these kinds does not amount to much in his world now. Apu hardly realizes that his own effort is a similar exercise in achieving personal excellence despite adverse circum-stances.

3-B Sarbojaya pines away to death

Back in Calcutta, he continues his study and work schedule. Sarbojaya's letter asks him to come home during a forthcoming holiday. She has not seen him for two months. She also offers to send some money if Apu needs it. Apu's reply gives the facile explanation that he has to study for a forthcoming examination and this will prevent him from coming home in the next holiday. Sarbojaya reads this reply and appears heartbroken. At this precise moment of her silent suffering a talkative woman neighbour drops in for a friendly visit. She starts off suggesting that Apu be married now to bring a daughter-in-law to look after Sarbojaya. Then she settles down to detail some scandalous family affairs on the silently suffering Sarbojaya.

In the evening, Sarbojaya sits under the tree, taking medicine. She is very ill. Nirupama comes in with fresh vegetables. She has informed Bhabataran about her illness. Sarbojaya insistently requests her not to write to Apu. He should come here only when he so wishes. Moreover, he should not be disturbed at his studies.

In Calcutta, Apu gets involved in the day routine of studies and printing press in the night. Sarbojaya continues to long for his visit. She is unwell but she would not allow Apu's studies to be disturbed by her illness.

When Sarbojaya receives this disappointing letter from Apu saying that he is not coming home, she is so much mentally lost that the continuous chatter of the neighbour woman about the scandals in her family hardly register with her. The situation is similar to the one in PP when Sarbojaya receives Harihar's first letter saying that he is not returning home since he has has not been able to make money. Sarbojaya simply sits down on the verandah step so much mentally lost that she is unaware of the baul mendicant at the door who is making repeated calls for alms. Durga saves the situation there by giving the alms to the mendicant.

The chattering neighbour suggests that Apu should marry so that Sarbojaya gets a help in her old age. This was a routine expectation from a marriage in traditional Indian society. Likewise, the neighbour's insensitivity to Sarbojaya's condition is typical of a situation in a norm - bound society – how individual nuances are not noticed.

It is a holiday and Apu has not gone home to the village. He is trying to catch up with studies. Apu and Shibnath chat on the Victoria Memorial grounds. Apu explains that he feels sleepy in the village. Instead of going there, has sent some money for mother out of the bonus from his job in the press. Shibnath offers him a cigarette. Apu refuses.

Back in Manasapota, Apu's sundial indicates it is evening. A very ill Sarbojaya sits gasping for breath as she sees in the distance the train passing by. This is the train which can bring Apu for her. She has hallucinations that he has arrived and she has heard him calling for her. She moves out of house looking for him at the poolside. In the gathering darkness all that she can see are numerous fireflies moving around in a dance. This is the last of her. The film avoids any details of her passing away.

Here we see a serious lack of judgment by Apu as also a change in his attitude. He has not gone home on this holiday due to pressure of studies here and also the dread of boredom in the village. Moreover, he suffers from the mistaken notion that money from him could compensate for his absence. Sarbojaya's longing is intensified by her awareness that the day was a holiday and Apu could have come to her.The hallucination triggered off by the evening train is the painful climax of her constant wait for Apu.

The dance of the fireflies, like the dance of the bugs on the ponds surface in PP, provides a meaningful visual pause before a major event. In PP, the dance of insects on the pool surface was an extension of the moment of happy expectation. Here, the fireflies dance at the sad climax of Sarbojaya's moment of intense frustration, which also leads to her death.

3-C Apu abandons priestly profession

Nirupama defies Sarbojaya's wishes and writes to Apu about mother's illness. As Apu returns by a train, the same vendor tries to sell him a balm which is a sure cure for all ills. Apu reaches home calling out for mother, moving from one door to the other through the empty courtyard. Then he sees the old man Bhabataran standing ominously, and realises that mother is no more. He sits down right there under a tree and cries to himself all alone.

At night Bhabataran tries to comfort the grieving Apu. He says that modern education is not for everyone and Apu could well stay on in Manasapota performing the job of a priest. However, Apu is grown up enough to take decisions. Next morning Apu decides to return immediately to Calcutta for studies. He begins sorting out mother's things to take along with him without waiting even the few days for mother's shradha, which he says would be performed at Kalighat. Bhabataran blesses the departing Apu who turns away even without bending to touch the old man's feet. He leaves with mother's mat and other things walking barefoot on the path away from the village, even as the distant clouds rumble.

Pather Panchali ends when Harihar gives up his long struggle to stay in the ancestral village, thereby snapping the social bonds and norms which had tied him to village life.

Aparajito ends when Apu finally

decides to abandon his ancestral profession, deliberately demonstrating, as if, his decision to the priest-granduncle by turning away from his blessings and even refusing to touch his feet. His decision is obviously taken in undue haste, since he has no alternative support system in the city. Sarbojaya's death is a sudden end to the distancing process of mother-son relationship. The Manasapota boy-priest had certainly grown up but merely into a Calcutta adolescent without any mature ability. Over the years, Sarbojaya, lonely in separation from Apu, had decayed fast to her eventual death one evening at the silent dark pond. The strain of silent distancing remains in suspension without finding any resolution, other than Sarbojaya's death.

This suspension is worked out in the reverse at the end of AS when Apu bonds with his son Kajal. Now the bonding is deliberate and conscious. Apu has been escaping it by blaming Kajal as the cause of Aparna's death. Now he realises that Kajal is continuation of his love for Aparna, and would find the fulfilment of his relation with Aparna in Kajal.

In PP the moving away from the village is an unwilling, forced act. In APJT the moving away from ancestral moorings is act of preference for an intense desire for a different, better life. In AS the father-son coming together is an act of trust between "friends."

APUR SANSAR

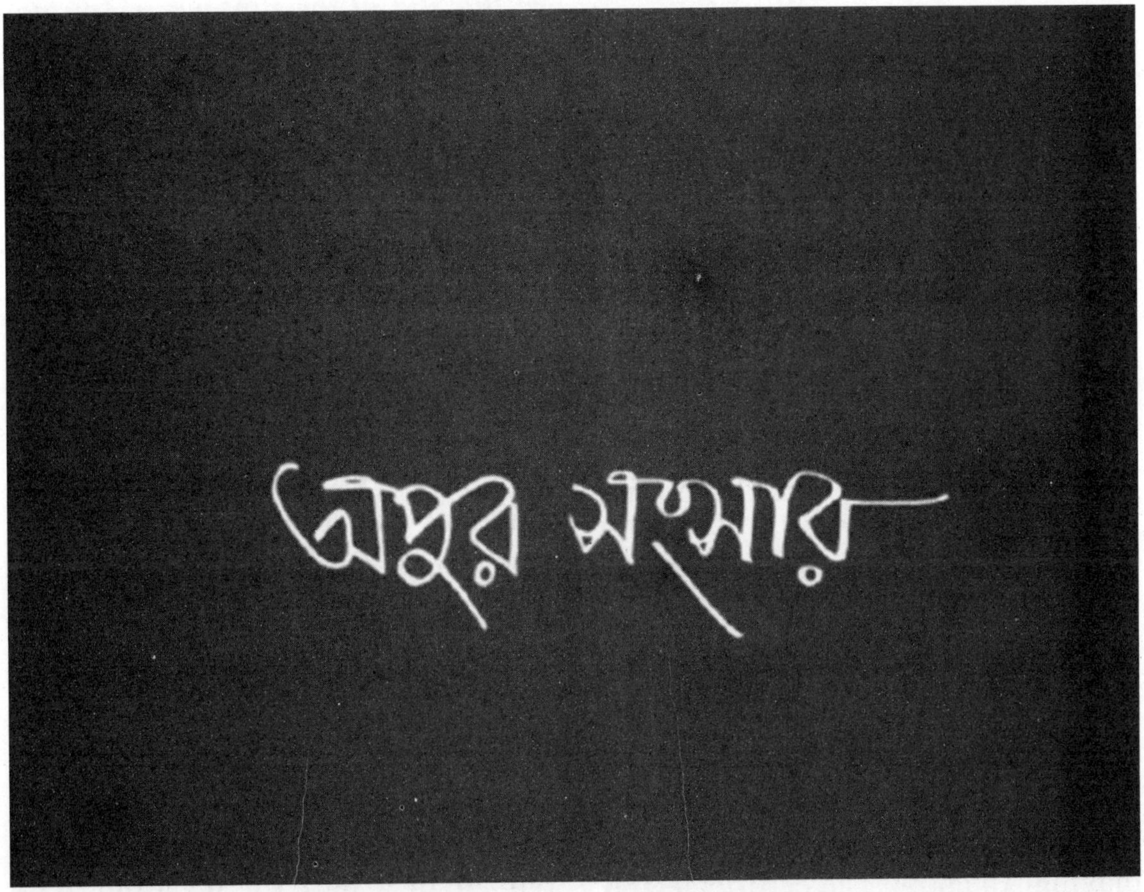

APJT ends with Sarbojaya's death. The last link with the family broken, Apu rejects the security of ancestral profession in Manasapota and goes on to continue studies in Calcutta.

AS is in three parts as follows:

Part 1 : Five years later, in Calcutta Apu is isolated, when Pulu pulls him out and takes him along to Khulna. In a sudden turn of chance events, Apu gets married to Aparna.

Part 2 : Apu's world of togetherness in happy marriage is shattered by Aparna's death in childbirth. Apu in depression isolates himself from the social world around and from his own creative work.

Part 3 : Six years pass. In Khulna, Apu's son, Kajal grows up devoid of any parental contact while Apu wanders around aimlessly. Pulu pulls him out of isolation again. Apu comes to see Kajal, tries and succeeds in bonding with the child.

APUR SANSAR – PART 1

Prologue

Some years have passed. The film begins when Apu, now about 22, cannot meet the expenses of his studies and is leaving college before completing his graduation. A professor has written out a certificate for Apu. The professor also says that Apu's article in the college magazine was of high quality and Apu could well consider taking up writing as a career. As Apu leaves the professor, we hear the slogans of a political procession on the street outside. The year would be around 1930.

This short scene is placed before the titles. The physical appearance of Apu at sixteen when we last saw him in APJT has changed considerably now at twenty two. A different actor is playing Apu now. The certificate and verbal exchange with the professor is a crisp introduction to the Apu of AS. After the titles, when he wakes up in the morning scene in his Calcutta room, everyone knows that that he is the grown up Apu.

The titles of the film fall into the design set for calligraphy of the Trilogy. Apu is already a writer. The titles are in the free flowing handwriting of a well educated person. The title music is detailed in Appendix on Music. The main segment of the title music is also used at the end of the film when Apu has found Kajal.

1-A Living in Isolation

1-A –(i) Morning - getting ready for the day

Like PP and APJT, AS also begins with a morning scene. Apu has a terrace room in a lowly three-storeyed residential building next to a railway shunting yard somewhere in Calcutta. It is raining, and the wind strains at the torn curtain of a room window. Fast asleep, Apu is woken up by the ringing alarm of the clock. He had been writing in his bed last night when he slept of. An ink bottle has spilt on the bedsheet. Apu removes the stained sheet and puts it in a pail for washing. The women down on the ground floor are complaining that the water tap is not running. The roof drain, however, makes a steady pour. Apu puts the bucket of stained sheet under the flow of rainwater. He enjoys being out in the rain, even doing some preliminary stretching for physical exercises as he enjoys getting drenched.

The torn window curtain had entered the narrative design of the Trilogy on the stormy night of Durga's death in PP. It appears again in the bachelor room in AS. When the newly married Aparna comes to this room, she gives an instant housewifely touch by replacing the damaged curtain by a proper one. Also, Apu's enjoyment of drenching here reminds us of his diffidence in getting wet in PP even while Durga revelled in the full impact of rain on her face and body.

Apu is shaving while interacting with the house owner who has come up demanding twenty one rupees as three months arrears for rent. Apu avoids any verbal confrontation by careful softening of the house owner's caustic observations and rude comments. However, the ultimatum to pay the due arrears by the evening is clearly conveyed. The house owner had also objected to electric illumination of the area where Apu was shaving. When he goes away, Apu switches on two more lights as if in mock revenge on the house owner.

While preparing to go out, Apu selects two of his books for pawning them presumably for the rent payment in the evening. A dried fern memento is discovered inside a book he is taking out. With obvious care, he saves the fern and places it in another book on the shelf.

Apu, now a struggling educated young person has this third storey terrace room for very sparse bachelor living. It is a bare, unsettled existence as can be seen in the torn window curtain and ink stained sheet, as also the unironed shirt under the sheet. He is hard pressed as the rent arrears indicate, but rather like Harihar he continues to have his aspirations, with pictures of scientists and literary masters on the walls. In contrast with his father Apu has started writing of some quality which is praised by his professor. His writing would be accepted for publication by a literary journal as he would gather from the letter he receives, and also later by Pulu when he reads the draft of the novel. He deflects the bitter sarcasm of the house-owner through good-natured humour, and also enacts the farce of mock vengeance by switching on more electric lights in daylight. His handling of the no-tap-water morning by prompt use of rainwater for washing and bathing indicates his improvisation skills and ability to be cheerful even in advrse circumstances.

In PP, Sarbojaya had great hesitation as she took out from a locked box an heirloom dish and bowl and took it out of the house for selling, taking care that no gossipy eyes notice her return to the house with food grain needed for the next round of survival. In AS Apu displays similar hesitation in selecting the two books which he has to sell for meeting the rent arrears.The emotional value of the sale of books is indicated by the presence of the fern leaf memento in one of the books.

As Apu goes down the stairs the neighbour women turn away their faces as a gesture of modesty. On the ground floor, a namesake, another A.K.Roy gives him a wrongly delivered letter. The neighbour talks lightheartedly about the possibility of a letter from a girl friend which could be misdelivered to him. Apu does not respond, and moves on. This letter from a literary magazine says that an article by Apu has been accepted for publication, which indeed is welcome news.

The quality of relations with neighbours has changed. The families around and the bachelor is an odd combination. After Apu's marriage, the neighbour women would get close to Aparna. Apu's namesake is light hearted about the entire institution of marriage as a threat to happy living. Apu's recognition as a writer is just about to begin. The writing is growing into the novel which he will discuss later with Pulu.In the urban environment, Apu is isolated in the heterogeneous neighbourhood.

1-A-(ii) Day- looking for a job

Apu now moves out searching for a job. Some children play cricket in the street. The ball hits Apu. A primary school needs a teacher. He goes inside. The old man who owns the school keeps on with the dice game he is playing even while talking to Apu. Apu is an Intermediate, but the school needs only a matriculate, that too on a salary of ten rupees. Next, at a medicine bottling shop, the owner has just one look at Apu to decide that he is unsuitable for working there. Apu is also repulsed by the sight of persons in a dark cramped space working on the mirthless job of sticking labels on small medicine bottles.

Apu's job hunt is on. But the kind of jobs that are available for a person with his qualification are neither paying, nor enjoyable.The Harimati Primary School has been in existence since 1895 for thirtyfive years. The school owner is so smug that he does not even bother to understand what Apu says. He goes on playing his dice game. We get another glimpse in yet another layer of the educational system, operating at the very minimal standard. This is very different from both the schools that Apu had attended.

The other job that Apu tries is the small scale bottling and labeling shop. There the working conditions are so cramped and dark that a clean sophisticated educated person would be stifled there. Even in his hard times, Apu cannot accept this as a workplace.

With education, the job possibilities have not improved. Apu had left his graduation midway and the hard times continue till Pulu promises him a job later.

1 (A) (iii) Evening - way back home

Coming back home on the tram after a frustrating day, Apu reinforces his morale by reading the letter about the acceptance of his article. He crosses the rail tracks in the shunting yard, jumps the fence in a shortcut to reach his building and goes up to his room. A girl at the window in the next building has been waiting for attention. He avoids her very scruplously, by carefully closing his window. Then he reclines on his bed, and plays the flute.

Apu needs some relief from the frustrations of living. He revels in the letter of acceptance received from the publisher and settles down to play the flute, losing himself in his music. Apu is very careful in avoiding the attention seeking girl by stealthily closing the window and keeping her out of sight. Aparna will also refer to this girl in a letter later. This short scene of Apu playing the flute is a pause between two events contrasted in their feeling tones. Apu's way of life has been laid out for us so far. Pulu's entry will initiate a new set of events.

Apu's escape in his own world is similar to Durga's escape into her world of Indir and kitten in the opening scene of PP. They are different in the age at which they withdraw in their worlds, but the pattern of protecting oneself from the onslaught of potential threat of frustration is similar.

The composition of the scene of Apu reading a letter in the tram followed by crossing the railway tracks while coming home will be repeated on the fateful evening when Apu receives the news of Aparna's death on reaching home.

1-(B) Pulu draws him out of isolation

His music is interrupted by the arrival of Pulu, a college friend. Pulu details out a long story of his efforts to trace Apu's whereabouts till he finally finds him here. He takes Apu out to a restaurant for dinner, a full meal after many days. Pulu persuades Apu to accompany him to Khulna for a wedding of a cousin, Aparna. After the meal, they go to a play. Returning from the play Apu recites a poem in a loud voice. Challenged by a policeman's voice, Apu tells him that they are the mythical figures. Apu talks of surviving without a job as a free creative person, while Pulu takes a more practical view of things. Apu is confident of his talent as a writer. He describes the novel he is writing which Pulu points out is almost autobiographical. Apu says that the love element in the novel will be provided by his imagination. Pulu argues that love cannot be imagined, it has to be experienced.

Apu is alone with no one in his family. Pulu, an old college friend, takes up a position of importance from this point in the plot. Their attachment is obvious from the account Pulu gives of his efforts to trace Apu. He also refers to being the first one to share many of the secrets as they were together in college. Looking at Apu's existence with rice and potato, a reminder of Sarbojaya's comment on the same food in PP, Pulu takes the decisions in his hands as it were and treats him to a good meal and plans to go with him to the marriage at Khulna.

The interaction with the policeman is in terms of the characters in the play they have watched (Sadhabar Ekadeshi by Deenbandhu Mitra) in which Mainak the Flying Mountain laments about his wings being clipped. The argument about role of imagination and experience shows the typical character of their friendship. There are free pricks to ego and reminders of early sharing that resume and revitalize the old bond. This relationship would grow through the film. Apu's interaction with Pulu is different from all the interactions shown so far which heightened Apu's isolation. Apu and Pulu share thoughts and feelings freely, and this helps to break Apu's isolation.

I-(C) Khulna till the marriage

Apu travels with Pulu in a small open boat to Khulna. Apu is taken in by the beauty around and plays the flute and recites a poem. Pulu reads the manuscript of Apu's novel and admires it profusely. They reach home where preparations for the wedding are in full swing. A special platform has been raised for the *shehnai* players. Apu is introduced to Pulu's uncle, the bride's father, and Murari, the younger son. He is a collegian. Pulu's aunt, the bride's mother is taken in by Apu's personality, comparing him to Krishna with a flute.

Inside the house, the bride's décor

is being completed. The aunt puts dots of white make up on her forehead, lining her brow.

On the river journey by boat, the tune of a Tagore song is played by Apu on the flute. Apu is enjoying the carefree travel and goes on to recite another Tagore poem. In the meanwhile, Pulu is reading Apu's manuscript of the novel and is all praise for it. Reaching the busy household as a surprise guest is a little awkward as he goes through the introductions. Pulu's reservations about the bridegroom and mother's response to Apu prepare the ground for later developments. Aparna, the bride, is almost through the bridal make-up in which her mother puts the finishing touch by lining her brows. In Ranu's marriage the bridal makeup was being done by friends and other women. Here, the bride's mother is personally supervising it, as she has prepared the daughter well for stepping into matrimony. The concern over bringing up the girl child as a cultural strand runs throughout the Trilogy. Here, Aparna will be seen fulfilling the grooming she has received.

The bridegroom's procession moves along the river towards the bride's house with the band playing : "He is a jolly good fellow." Apu is sleeping under a tree oblivious of all the activity. The bridegroom suffers uncontrolled body movements and would not come out of his palanquin at the bride's house despite persuasion by several relatives. When he eventually does tumble out, his condition is evident to everyone around. He is insane. The bride's father tries to cover up the groom's behaviour. However, Aparna's mother is entirely firm in protecting the daughter from an unsuitable marriage. However, the hour of Aparna's marriage tonight is astrologically fixed and if that auspicious time slips by, she will remain unmarried forever.

This mismatch of the proposed marriage brings out the strength of Aparna's mother as also the father's attitude who makes it an issue of personal prestige and belief in the superstition, irrespective of the daughter's future. This points to several cultural associations of the way marriages were arranged in a traditional society. Aparna's mother, on the other hand is indignant and she is determined to protect her daughter from any mismatched matrimony. She pushes her own husband out of the door and bolts it against him.

The Trilogy portrays the inner strength of women in several facets. It is displayed in decisions and actions of Sarbojaya, for example her grit of holding the children during Harihar's absence with a firm base in the norms of good behaviour, and her insistence on protecting Harihar's reputation when Indir acts to tarnish it, or her own repelling of Nandababu's advances, or her instant decision to leave Benaras in interest of Apu's upbringing. Here, Aparna's mother protects her daughter with the same strength, with a firm refusal for the unsuitable match. Aparna uses the same strength in a soft and sweet mode when she prevents Apu from increasing expenses later in their household in Calcutta.

Apu is away from the bustle of the marriage, sleeping under a tree on the riverside. He does not notice the arrival of the bridegroom's party. A member of the family led by Pulu approach Apu, still under the tree, and make the proposal of marriage to him. Apu is repelled by the very idea as if it belongs to the Middle Ages. The appeal to him is in the terms of the bride's future and the prestige of the family. However, later, he thinks he would be doing something noble in saving the prestige of the family and he changes his mind. Pulu helps him out promising to fix a job for him in Calcutta, and also take care of his immediate requirements like a clean kurta to be worn as the bridegroom.

The father, with his belief in astrology had no choice in the matter and agreed, however reluctantly. At the marriage ritual, the mother receives favourable comments from a relative, and she talks of her premonition at the first meeting of Apu.

The traditional belief system was that the two families getting united by the marriage should match in economic and social prosperity. Here, Apu had no parental family and he had nothing to fall back on as the provider of the new family responsibility. But the crisis had to be urgently resolved. The marriage ceremony is quickly performed, and Apu meets the approval of the bride's mother. The belief system around omens, premonitions and astrological prescriptions runs a full circle here. For Apu this marks a point of sudden change from his isolated life in Calcutta into the practical responsibilities of married life.

In the bridal chamber, Apu paces the floor anxiously. He needs to know that the bride Aparna has accepted him with full knowledge of his family and economic situation. Aparna softly agrees and tells him that Pulu has told her that he is a writer. A song of the boatman is heard in the air. Apu decides that Aparna will accompany him to Calcutta to face the new life.

This scene indicates Apu's approach to the marriage relationship. He is keenly aware of the gap between his situation and Aparna's background. Apu wants Aparna to be fully aware of his condition and her life ahead. He wants to be sure that she too accepts the bond. Their interaction sets the tone of trust and transparency in their relationship. It is awkward that they have stayed on in the bride's house and he wants her to come to Calcutta with him.

The boatman's song has a forward association with the scene some six years later, when Apu trie to be friendly with Kajal in the same room with the same song out on the river.

This part of the film begins with Apu's isolation and ends in togetherness.After all the struggle in his Aparajito years, he was full of enthusiasm and hope but was subdued by the circumstance. Pulu's friendship took him to Khulna and to his marriage. Aparna was ready to complement him even when their familial and social backgrounds were sharply contrasted.

APUR SANSAR – PART 2

Apu and Aparna reach their residence in Calcutta in a hackney carriage. As they climb up the stairs stealthily, none of the neighbours notices them. Apu takes her to the room where she sits on the window sill and sees through a hole in the curtain, a mother and child. Apu notices as she wipes her tears and checks with her if she is alright and takes her down to meet the women of the building who welcome her as a bride.

The Calcutta house offers a sharp contrast to the elegant bride. Aparna sits on the window sill and watches the road below through the hole in the curtain. We have been watching holes and curtains in PP. On the morning of the first day to school, Apu is woken up by Durga as she sees his open eye through a hole in the chadar and tickles him to get up. Here, Aparna's sobs at her first experience of her Calcutta home are controlled by seeing a mother and child in the pavement below through the hole. This torn curtain will be changed by Aparna as she takes up the housewifely duties with full authority.

The torn curtain has been replaced. It is morning. Apu and Aparna sleep in bed and the alarm clock rings sharply. Aparna wakes up hastily and tries to move, but finds that her sari end is tied to Apu's sheet. She unties the knot and slaps Apu playfully and goes to the door. As she tries to light the coal stove, Apu wakes up in the bed and fondly handles a hairpin he finds on

Aparna's pillow. Apu reaches for his cigarette pack and he finds in it a note from her reminding him that he has to smoke only one cigarette after the meal. Apu smiles as he puts the packet back. As he keeps on watching her at work she objects to his staring saying that she is not new here. The stove is ready. She starts breaking chunks of coal as a cockroach creeps out and is promptly killed. Apu comes out playing the flute, while Aparna wipes the sweat from her forehead and carries the stove to the terrace. The sharp whistle of a railway engine in the yard below hurts her ears. Apu stops playing and is worried if she would be repenting the marriage. They talk about it and Aparna gets ready for the bath and Apu says he will go out and look for a servant. Aparna prevents him from increasing any such expenses. She also requests him to give up the tuition he has at present to be able to spend more time with her.

The portrayal of the happy married life has several aspects. Aparna has taken up the routine efficiently and Apu has started working out his romantic dream. Aparna has also taken up the task of keeping Apu's smoking under control. He responds by not smoking at that time. The little romantic prank is offset immediately by the practical daily

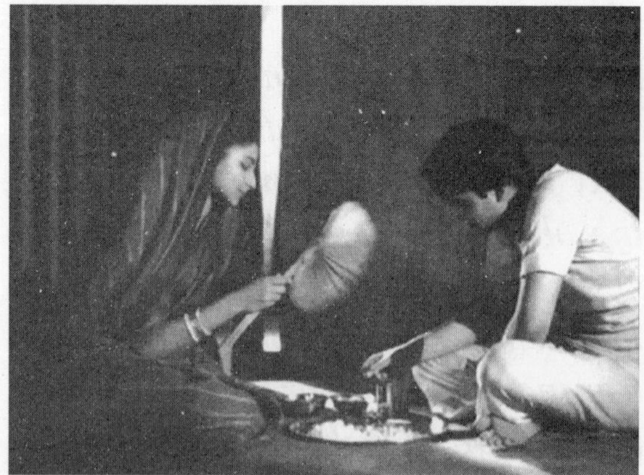

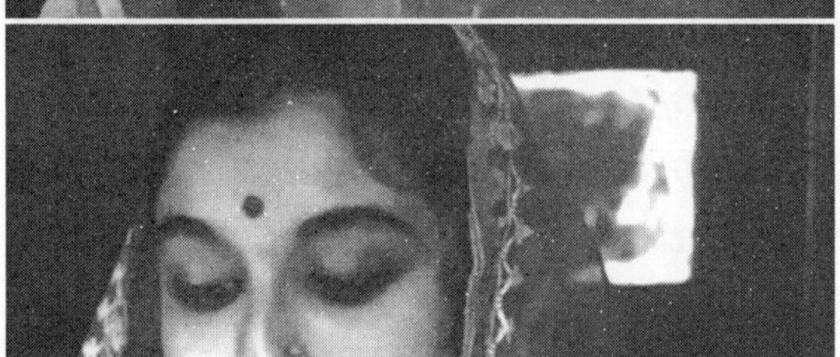

chore of lighting the coal stove. Apu's concern at seeing Aparna work makes him think that she might be regretting this marriage. Aparna, on the other hand, points out that for paying for a maid Apu would need to be away longer from the house for making money. She would rather want him to give up the existing tuition so that he can spend more time with her. In Khulna, Apu and Aparna had started with trust and transparency. Here we see them working it out in the day–to-day sensitivity to each other's needs. Apu's flute is not an escape now; it is a celebration of his happiness. The noisy shunting yard or the limited money Apu earns are considered secondary by Aparna to the value of their togetherness.

In the evening Aparna waits for Apu, and plans a prank with a welcome bang. She blows up a paper bag and waits to surprise him when he comes up. They enjoy the moment. At the evening meal Aparṇa fans as Apu eats and then, reciprocally, a sleepy Apu fans as Aparna eats. Another night, Apu teaches her English from a primer. She recites a few spellings and meanings of English words. Apu wants to go to bed, but she insists on learning some more.

Another evening, Apu takes her to

the cinema where a mythological film is being screened. Apu is bored but she is involved. On return, he hires a hackney carriage. Aparna is pregnant and shortly she is going for her delivery at the mother's house and Apu wants to enjoy every moment with her. He tells her that he has not written anything in the last few months but now is going to complete writing the novel and dedicate it to his wife. In these tender moments Aparna even lights a cigarette for Apu. As he comments on her eyes, she avoids escalation of romance by a tactful answer.

As Apu sets up his world, several subtle details of happiness in marriage are now displayed which involve fun and responsibility,with adequate opportunity to Aparna to play in her own contribution. The complementary nuances in this relationship can be seen in several pranks, like the surprise with the paper bag, the mutual fanning at mealtime, and the delay in going to bed as Aparna insists on learning more English words. Such fun has enormous flexibility. The private space of the hackney carriage gives Aparna opportunity to continue the benign fun. Apu's remark about knowing the meaning of the word 'wife' sums up the intense quality of their relationship. She even lights up an out of routine cigarette for Apu. This too, is an aspect of their flexibility. Despite differences, their life together is full of joy since their relationship has no trace of power and control that characterizes a male dominated marriage. The word "kajal"(kohl) gets emphasised here. The expected son will be named Kajal. The name of the child has a backward association with this happy moment.

The life of togetherness of Apu and Aparna is portrayed by a series of actions which explore the essence of love as it is lived. The details of everyday actions glow with the visible energy of articulations of love. The strong bond of marital relation holds the symmetry : He does this; She does that. However, He and She have freedom to do this or that in their preferred manner. This is modernity which is not rejection of tradition but a redefinition of the eternal values of the family. The strength lies in the shared value of togetherness and the freedom lies in the choices that are open.

The parting scene at the railway station. The train is due to depart. Aparna is inside the train while Apu is on the platform. They are speechless. As the whistle is blown and the train starts moving, Aparna suddenly has several last minute instructions for Apu. The train leaves and Apu is left all alone.

It is time for the pregnant Aparna to go to her mother's house for her delivery. Apu would never have let Aparna go, but the circumstances force it on him. Referring to the railway motif in the Trilogy, the parting scene here presents the railways as a system that separates Apu from his beloved in the same manner as in APJT, the railways had separated Apu from his mother leaving her in loneliness. The shape of this scene expresses the difficulty and pain for Apu. She is already in the compartment of the train, Apu has the sense of being left alone on the platform. Moments slip by and the whistle blows, signalling departure. Aparna's pent-up speechlessness in the public space of a railway carriage is released in a sudden flow not about matters of the heart, but instructions of practical trivialities. As Aparna is carried away by the train Apu tries to move with it. However, separation is the bitter fact of the situation. Apu is left alone on the platform.

Apu is at his office job. Apu sits staring out of the window with some unfinished material standing on the typewriter. A colleague comments on Apu's happiness in marriage and compares his own obedient and uninteresting wife with Apu's wife whom he has not seen. Sheltered by the typewriter, Apu reads Aparna's letter complaining about the one less than the number of letters he had promised to write. As he travels by a tram, he reads the letter again where she mentions the girl in the neighbouring building and asking him to keep the window closed. He walks home happily and on the way, he picks up a crying child and takes it to the mother. He has some interaction with his namesake Mr. Ray regarding the family.

While Aparna is away Apu's days drag on, but happily interspersed with Aparna's sweet letters. At work, his colleague notices that he is happily married and complains about his own excessively obedient wife. This observation is marginal here, yet it refers to the process of bringing up a girl child to be an eventual good wife. The element of fear of husband's authority leads to excessive obedience and in the process the wife becomes uninteresting. The contrast between the two marriages brings out the uniquely individuated character of Apu and Aparna as a couple. Apu's private world is held close by him and Aparna and no one else.The private space of matrimonial relationship is created by individuals as they fulfill their dreams of togetherness. They observe public norms, yet the inner reality lights up their life and it can be noticed by others. The exchange of letters is their means of keeping the continuity of togetherness even when they are physically separated.

As he goes upstairs, he finds Murari waiting on the terrace. He has brought the unhappy news of Aparna's death in childbirth. Apu loses control and hits him hard and then collapses on his bed.

This point serves a devastating blow to the world he had created. He was still in the process of making it his haven. It moves to a sudden and total destruction with the news of Aparna's death. He gets violent first and hits Murari in his agitation, but immediately afterwards collapses completely entirely unaware of the world around him.

Here we can notice a significant device used in the Trilogy. A scene is done in terms of the reaction to the event rather than the event itself. Aparna's death is offscreen. The blow received by Apu from Aparna's death is physically passed on to Murari with such suddenness that it becomes the central event and the spectator feels the quality of the blow of death.The upsurge of violence is followed by a long period of total collapse. PP has a similar construction of intense emotional outburst and the collapse. Shejobou charges Durga of an offsreen theft of Tunu's bead necklace. This results in sudden violence as Sarbojaya punishes Durga severely, and then after the violence herself collapses in exhaustion for a long time.

Apu had responded to deaths in the family and ultimately he was isolated till he built his world with Aparna. In case of Durga's death and the later discovery of the necklace, it was handled by him by keeping the dead sister's secret. In case of the mother, he severed his bonds with the family profession. But Aparna's death is a blow that throws him from the blissful togetherness into the abyss of isolation. Now, for him the very nucleus of his existence has exploded and this shatters him completely. He is oblivious of the child; and as we know later, he had blamed the child for Aparna's death.

Time passes by senselessly for Apu. As he continues to mourn a neighbour woman, Pintu's mother, brings food for him. She talks about Aparna's sweet manners. She suggests that Apu could always marry again. Apu is lost in his grief and does not seem to react to anything.

Apu is inconsolable. The kind of closeness Aparna had developed with the neighbours becomes apparent here. The suggestion of a second marriage for Apu brings out the gap between Apu's condition and the social expectation under such circumstances. Apu in grief does not eat adequately. The second marriage also implies the need of someone to run the household. The neighbours cannot look after him indefinitely. Apu's views regarding marriage are different from the general social expectations. He had found his own unique expression of togetherness and joy. It is the deepest individualized concern that Apu has developed in the process of his personal growth.

A clock ticks in the background as Apu strains himself to get up. As Apu sees himself in the mirror the clock stops ticking and a distant train whistle is heard. He goes down and stands by a track on which a train is coming on. He hears the train whistle. He has possibly contemplated suicide, but retracts at the last moment. A pig is hurt by the train.

Apu is struggling to get back to reality even if it is bleak. A train whistle on a face is a compositional device used in the Trilogy at points of important decisions. The device is used on Harihar in PP on the night he decides to abandon Nischindipur and go to Benares, and on Sarbojaya in APJT when she decides to leave Benares and go back to a village in Bengal. In Apu's case here, he goes out to the railtrack with possibly suicide in mind. However, as the engine moves closer, a pig is hurt by the moving train. The pig's squealing sound detracts attention.The critical moment has passed. Apu keeps standing as the train hurtles by. Compositionally, it reminds of PP when Apu had experienced a train for the first time It was the indifferent massive train in the foreground and small, curious Apu in the background. Here, Apu is in the foreground with his massive pain and the train hurtles by indifferently.

Apu writes a letter to Pulu saying that he is leaving in search of freedom. He is taking the manuscript of the novel with him. Apu takes off on a train. A variation of the Apu theme music runs in the background till the end of the sequence on the sunrise at the hilltop.

Apu's condition and the subsequent isolation seems to separate him from all social contact. But Apu writes a letter to Pulu that he is leaving Calcutta for a wandering in search of freedom. Though he calls it freedom, it is quite clear that it is aimless. We see him on a train as he begins his free wandering. Apu's purposeful train journeys from Manasapota to Calcutta were very different from this aimless travel. He leaves with an impulse to move away. It is not the destination but the pull away from here and now.

At Aparna's house, baby Kajal lies in a cradle and Aparna's mother sits by, sighing. Apu is on a beach. He has grown a beard and he is still footloose.

This aimless wandering is a long period as we notice Aparna's mother with baby Kajal. She too is inconsolable but has the responsibility of the baby. As a grandmother, Aparna's mother continues to care for the baby as the daughter's death has passed on the natural responsibility to her. Apu, lost in his grief, has not connected with the child at all.

Apu's wandering to the beach gives him no solace and deepens his grief further. He is still looking for his freedom in vain.

Apu is moving through all kinds of locales, the hills and the forests and stops to feel a fern and moves on in despair. One day on a hilltop as the sun rises, he takes out the pages of the manuscript of his novel and throws them away to the wind and to the wilderness.

Apu's depression leads to the ultimate renunciation of his ambitions. He has no interest in living or achievements as he lets go the manuscript pages of his novel to the wind, his creative work that he had dedicated to Aparna. With this act, he disconnects himself entirely from the world of social relations.

The second part of the film moves from intense togetherness to complete isolation for Apu.

APUR SANSAR – PART 3

Years have passed by. Kajal, Apu's son, now six years old, walks through the trees with a mask on and a catapult in his hand. He aims with it and approaches a dead bird. Pulu,now back from his stay abroad, sees it all as Kajal carries the dead bird tied to a string. A woman is sitting under a tree frying fritters. Kajal lowers the dead bird in front of the woman who screams in fear, while Kajal runs away with some fritters. An elderly passerby tries to intervene. Kajal bites him in the hand and engages with him in a snappy verbal exchange in which Kajal talks of his father who lives in Calcutta.

The grandfather complains to Pulu about Kajal's wild behaviour. When the grandmother was alive she could handle Kajal. But the grandfather cannot control the wild mischief of the child. Pulu enquires about Apu's address in some colliery near Nagpur.

The practical difficulty created after Aparna's death is sensed by Pulu as he notices Kajal with a mask and the dead bird, wandering alone, playing mischief with the woman frying fritters and talking back to the elderly man. Kajal has pent up tensions.The absence of his parents is unexplained. In his childish manner, Kajal believes that his father lives in Calcutta and is annoyed with him for some reason and left him alone. His immediate experience is of the aged grandfather who would maintain discipline by wielding the beating stick. Thus he lacks the very stability of a family surrounding in which children learn as they grow. He does not have playmates to form a children's world for practising social interaction.

Pulu sees the condition of the child and senses all this situation.The child needs parental contact and care. Pulu senses the failure of Apu to provide emotional support to the child and decides to go and meet him.

Placing of the six years gap towards the end of Apur Sansar is an aspect of the design of Trilogy. In each of the films, the gap takes us across some patch of living in the pattern that has been set. In case of this film, Apu's isolation is oblivious of the growing child and we see the effect of the neglect.It suggests the need for emotional bonding with Kajal.

Apu moves along a path in the mining area as Pulu catches up with him. They exchange preliminary notes as they walk. Apu has this job here for the mere need of earning for meals. He has thrown away his novel, and he is ultimately saving up to go out of the country. Pulu reminds him about Kajal. Apu needs to understand that he has a duty as a father to bring up the child. He has been sending some money now and then, but that is not adequate. The child needs parental care.

Apu offers to provide for the child by sending more money but Pulu is not satisfied and insists that Apu accepts active responsibility of bringing up the child. At the emotional height of the interaction, Apu breaks down in pain as he lets out the true reason for his aversion: it is because Kajal lives that Aparna did not live. Pulu, of course, has no method to handle this argument, and he leaves having sufficiently aroused Apu's awareness of his son and his responsibility to bring him up.

Pulu now functions as a friend with a full-fledged definite plan. He is involved with Apu's past tragedy, and now in his future. The child has to be saved from growing up into a vagabond. He is very firm with Apu, not giving him the space to nurse his grief anymore. Apu has started thinking about going to some foreign country without realising that he has some unfinished business here. Pulu pulls him to that responsibility first. After Apu reveals his inner accusation of the child as the cause of Aparna's death, Pulu leaves him to take up his own decisions in the matter of shouldering the responsibility as a father. When Apu talks of Aparna's death, in the background you hear the music related to Harihar's death in APJT.

The shape of this interaction is very different from the friendly interactions we have seen so far. Pulu has a definite purpose and Apu perhaps continues to expect Pulu to support him emotionally. The crisp and clear message that Apu has to take charge of bringing up his son is harsh on Apu who is still tender with the injury he nurses. Pulu just stays long enough to rouse him out of his grief and depression and leaves, forcing Apu to take the initiative.

Apu comes to Khulna. The old man standing in the verandah does not recognise him. He introduces himself. The old man responds with some sarcasm asking if he had come to take Kajal away. Apu says that he may arrange for Kajal in Nishchindipur. The old man directs Apu upstairs for Kajal, who had been unwell but was now improving.

Apu goes up to the upstairs room where Kajal is sleeping in one side of the big double bed. Apu waits uneasily in a chair by the window, the boatman's song floats on the air again and brings back memories of that momentous night with Aparna. Apu gets close to sleeping Kajal and places his hand very tenderly on Kajal's forehead. Kajal wakes up, rolls off the bed, runs away out of the room and out of the house. Apu calls after him, but in vain.

Apu follows him out in the courtyard upto the gate, repeating "I am your father." Kajal looks back angrily and throws a stone aimed at Apu. Apu ducks and saves himself. However, the old man is annoyed and wants to punish Kajal. He raises his walking stick to bring it down heavily on Kajal, but Apu prevents him by holding his arm in mid-air exclaiming that this would kill the child. Kajal watches this solemnly, but runs away from Apu all the same.

Apu has brought a toy rail engine for Kajal. Kajal, however, rejects the gift and throws it back to Apu instantly. At night Apu tries to sleep by Kajal's side, and make some conversation around the promise of numerous fairy stories. Kajal refuses to accept any gestures of affection.

Next morning, Apu gets ready to leave. He hands over Aparna's jewellery to grandfather. and says that he would arrange with Pulu to send Kajal to a boarding school. Apu refuses to consider the suggestion that he exercises the right of the father of the child and forcibly take him away.

Apu leaves, walking away from the house along the path by the river. He becomes aware that Kajal is standing near the house in an expectant pose watching Apu go away. Apu halts and turns asking Kajal if he wants to say something. A short verbal exchange follows. Kajal would come with Apu who will go to Calcutta and take Kajal to his "father". The "father" wil not be cross with Kajal and not leave him again. Apu identifies himself as a "friend." In the meanwhile Grandfather has also come up calling for Kajal. Apu encourages Kajal, assuring him that grandpa would not know. Kajal makes a short run. Apu picks up Kajal in his arms and perches him on his shoulders and they move along the path. The musical background at this point to the end is interesting. The run of the child is covered by Mother's Wail and finally the Apu theme comes on. Grandfather watches from a distance holding the rejected toy railway engine as he turns to go back to the house. Kajal is perched on Apu's shoulders and they move away together.

The interaction of Apu and Kajal develops through several distinct stages. Apu comes to the house in Khulna. Grandfather puts Apu directly in contact with Kajal. It is up to Apu to connect with the child.

Apu does make efforts and fails. In the room, when Apu touches Kajal's forehead however tenderly, he is repulsed. The repulsion is stronger, Kajal throws a stone at him.Apu's act of holding the grandfather's hand is a very strong signal for Kajal. But he quietly watches Apu, trying to make sense of this stranger.This act of kindness seems to have made some impression on Kajal. But that is not adequate. The effort with toys and promise of stories does not make progress and Kajal continues to keep his distance.

When Apu starts to leave, the suggestion that Apu asserts his authority as father and take Kajal away by force is unacceptable. However, at the last moment, Kajal is willing to trust Apu as a "friend" who will take him to his "father" in Calcutta, with the assurance that the father will not be cross and leave him alone again. A segment of the music Mother's Wail is placed against Kajal's short run towards Apu. The Trilogy ends with Kajal perched on Apu's shoulders as they move triumphantly ahead against the Apu Theme music in the background. The mother's wail covers Kajal's run. It was withheld as it were and now when he decides to trust, it is let out in the expression built into the run.The triumph of life and assertion of the human bond end the Trilogy on a note of hope and optimism.

The simple narrative of the Trilogy is dense as we have seen and the key to unravel it lies in watching the details with the concept of the three layered structure in mind.There is no detail that occurs by chance or without purpose.As a work of Art the Apu Trilogy stands unique in its integrity.

Chapter 4

EPILOGUE

2009 is the 50th year of the completion of the Apu Trilogy, three films of high excellence and acclaim, while two of them, PP and AS were popular success as well with Bengali audiences. These films have also triggered off an ongoing debate : Mass entertainment fim vs.film as a work of Art. The arguments have been manifested in numerous variations, from snides and sniggers to overheated printed pages to irresponsible statements in the Indian Parliament. Since the focus of this study is The Apu Trilogy as a work of film Art, we could sum up the main issues of this debate. **A work of film Art differs from the entertainment formula film. In what manner? Can we get a historical perspective on this issue?**

Let us take 1895, the year of the Lumiere projection as the beginning of Film. Three kinds of persons were attracted to the new gadgetry, the financier businessman, the skilled technician and the Artist. Film was good investment for the financier, who could foresee the potential entertainment need of audiences which would develop with the rapid urbanisation all around in the beginning of the 20th century. However, film making involved complicated machinery and processes which could be handled only by skilled technicians. Thus the financier and the skilled technician combined to set up the film industry for making entertainment films for the emerging mass audiences. The Artist, deliberately spelled here with capital A, knew all the technical aspects of film making well enough. However, he wanted to explore how this technique could express a vision of life which was different from the entertainment formula of the industry. Naturally, the Artist would find no support from the industry and and he had to wait impatiently and forage around for making his film.

The financier- technician combine set up Hollywood so confidently that within twenty years of the invention of the camera, by 1915-16, D.W.Griffith could make "The Birth of a Nation" and "Intolerance," full-length spectacles with battle scenes, huge sets and all the paraphernalia of multimllion dollar extravaganza.The new technology was also exported out fast. D.G. Phalke financed "Raja Harishchandra" in 1912 with his own money to demonstrate that films could be made here in India as well. Immediately the financier-skilled technician combination appeared here as well, and kept on developing through the decades in many phases, to self-styled kinship as Bollywood, and with the national production numbers the largest in the world, and in numerous languages in the vast cultural mosaic of India.

Let us get back to basics. In bare terms, **the film camera is a recording machine** which can make a visual record of anything in movement, be it nascent events like a baby at breakfast or a train entering a station to the ongoing complications of a slumdog earning his millions. **Likewise, the sound-mike-machinery** could make a record of any aural event like a greeting: "Good morning, Mr. Edison" or recitation of wiser words: "To be or not to be, that is the question..." What we need to celebrate is that **for the FIRST Time in Human History,** cinematography made it possible to record any visual movement and reproduce it as an image of life-like accuracy on a screen. The life-like experience of the Lumiere image had the press break out in applause : "It is life itself !" and the cinema was promptly named Vitagraph or Biograph. Likewise, for the first time in human history, the sound-mike-machinery made it possible for any sound to be recorded and reproduced at convenience. Cinematography and audiography combined ten years after "The Birth of a Nation" to give birth to the sound film.

In essence, **film making is narration with moving visual images and sound**. **Two types of films are possible** depending how the camera-mike is used for film composition. In one case the camera-mike is used for its recording-reproducing power. In the second case, the camera-mike is used for its expressive power.The first case is of a film which applies the recording power of the camera-mike machines to the resources of the older arts like Literature, Theatre, Music and Dance by recording elements invoving script, director, actor, dialogue, set, property, makeup and costume, song and dance and digital effects, and then, in essence, reproduce them. The second kind of film essentially uses the resources of cinematography like visual composition and the resources of audiography like sound design and two combined by rerecording as audio-visual composition to create the basic narrative units of film. In the second case too, the film maker uses the resources of the older arts like script, director, actor, dialogue, set, properties, makeup and costume, song and dance. However, each one of them is subject to the discipline of film composition. For example, acting and dialogue delivery for a closeup has to be different from acting for a long shot. Likewise, the lighting and makeup of an actor or a set will essentially be controlled by the camera position, which in turn will depend on the detail of the shot in the shooting script. **And more importantly, in a work of art the narrative surface has an underpinning layer of feeling and meaning which becomes palpable when we probe the density of composition**. In this book we have constantly pointed out the density in various elements in the composition in the films. We have also explored how the structure of the narrative and the meaning of the film are inter-dependent.The expressive structure created by the Artist articulates the inarticulable aspects of the life of feeling.

There are **three essential differences** between a popular entertainment film and a work of film Art. **One is the disposability of parts**. A popular entertainment film is usually a mixture of entertainment elements strung along a narrative. Hence, if you remove that scene, or this fight, this romantic interlude or this comic segment, a song, or a dance, the film will still hold withot losing its essential story. On the contrary, a work of film Art is one organic whole, in which each part is in multiple relationships with other parts. Thus, if you remove a part you would be removing a vital part which is contributing to the whole film. The analysis of the films of the Apu Trilogy has revealed the numerous relationships between the parts which hold the films together as a whole.

The entertainment film reduces the complex matters in actual life to simplified versions. This is **the second characterstic** of a popular entertainment film. Take for instance, the human character. Each person is a complex individual. **The popular cinema reduces the human characters in film plots to stereotypes** like the hero, the heroine, the villain, and character types like the mother, the mother-in-law, the faithful family servant ..... you know them from hundreds of films you have seen. Likewise, relations like friendship or mother-son relationship, or any other, are reduced in popular film to a simplified single point affairs. This device of reduction to stereotype also reduces complications. The point is easily made for the audience, like the villain must look like a villain, have villainous intention for the hero, or the hero must be in love with the heroine. Any subtle complications of the kind which occur in real life situations are avoided in the film plot. The stereotype character is the precise negation of the character in depth which the Artist creates. In effect, the popular film maker does not take any risks with the audience. The stereotype characters and situations ensure that what he is saying in uncomplicated terms is readily understood by the audience. In contrast, the artist takes the risk that the spectator may find it difficult to understand the characters and the situations without thinking. That is, the characters and situations in the film persuade you to think. And,when you think about the problem in the film, you think in terms of your own experience of life. This is precisely the social function of all great works of fiction. **A good film or novel or short story makes you more sensitive and sharpens your awareness of life**. The popular stereotyped film reduces the complexity of life and seduces you not to think about life and its problems and work towards their solution. In this sense, the popular film lulls sensibility rather than sharpen it as the work of Art does.

The third characterstic of the popular film is that it is full of the good things of life, handsome men and women to look at, pretty locations, handsome houses, with pretty furniture and curtains. The rule for visual composition in popular film is that anything that enters the frame should be good to look at, it should be easy on the eyes, the humans in the foreground or elements in the background. Take, for instance, the image of the woman. Irrespective of character, the woman would be lighted up in a manner to reveal and heighten sexuality. The heroines put on no clothes but costumes. Quite often she dresses to reveal. Similarly, things in the interiors, consumer goods like food, clothes, furniture, curtains, or fittings like balcony with the circular staircase, and in the outdoors, cars, interior of aeroplanes,... and places of tourist or religious interest,....add on....The film appears as if designed to seduce the spectator to desire those consumer goods. Most film makers work within this duplex formula: Reduce and Seduce.

Some film makers do tell stories of socially conscious themes but continue to remain within the entertainment framework by providing within the same film two kinds of ingredients; **speakable elements** which the spectator can talk about when approving the film, and also **unspeakables**, that the spectator does not talk about but enjoys all the same. In such films quite often the relationship deals between two persons suffering due to a social difference like for instance a man-woman love made impossible due to difference of high-low caste. The problem in such films are solved by coincidences, or an accident or death. The popular entertainment film provides **a pleasure packet of life made easy** and its existence is sustained by mass audience acceptance of dream solutions of real problems.

METAPHORIC CONNECTIONS

There are several **metaphoric connections across the body of the Trilogy which carry meanings beyond their obvious surface connotations.They create an opening into other areas of life of feeling which lead us far beyond the mere narrative of the Trilogy.** Take one example of such a metaphoric relation. One dominant factor in Harihar Ray's existence is the enforced uprooting of his life. He wanted to hold on to the ancestral village but simply could not do so. He had to pack up his meagre belongings, abandon his house and leave on a bullock cart. However, Nishchindipur also has a train hooting across the peaceful countryside which is put there in the film not merely as a spectacle for the children on an adventurous outing. These two elements, the bullock cart in the foreground story and the train and the railway system in the background environment resonate with meanings, since they continue to appear consistently over the events in Trilogy. Let's see how. Historically, the train and the railway system came on the Indian scene in early 19th century with the British Raj along with other systems of administrative power. The Trilogy story is placed in early 20th century, the Benares segment is dated 1920. The railways were a facility for mobility. They brought people together, letting new relationships to emerge. In the Trilogy the trains are the vehicle of separation of characters, of families and locales and also of social togetherness.The metaphor works this way. In PP, Apu's small face is seen against the roaring mass of the moving train. The small-big differential working at the level of power and at the level of economy are expressively equivalent to the huge machine as it thunders across and the small human face. Investment in the railways is a political and economic decision to control the lives of the Indian people. It meant jobs, new technical skills and also a device for speedy travel. The quiet kans flower flecked countryside has been polluted by the dark industrial smoke. The train changes the look of the countryside and dominates the landscape at all points. As a minor instrument of the Raj the passing steel girders of the railway bridge at Benares sweep across the river front view even of the ancient city of Kashi on the eternal mother Ganga. Our first entry into Calcutta is through the monstrously bleak approach vista of rail tracks into Sealdah terminus station with Apu's train moving in along one of the lines. In Apur Sansar Apu lives next to a railway siding where the sounds and smoke of the engines dominate the environment. The loud engine whistle annoys the delicate Aparna who is accustomed to the boatman's melodious song on the river. And, for the grieving Apu after Aparna's death, the whistle is the signal for the urge to die, and the shunting railway engine is the immediately available lethal device. On several occasions in the Trilogy, the train separates the suffering individuals. In Manaspota the railway track on the back door horizon is an ever present cause of anxiety in Sarbojaya's mind of the increasing distance between her and Apu. The train whistle sound is placed on the face of characters at decisive moments. The placing of the railways in relation to the main story changes as the story unfolds. In Nischindipur it is somewhere far out there, its sound and whistle can be heard in the night, but when Apu sees it one afternoon, it is a monstrous force. The train brings Harihar's family into Benares, and some time later would also take the severely decimated family out of Benares. In Manaspota, the rail track on the distant horizon was a constant warning to Sarbojaya of her inevitable seperation from Apu brought nearer with every morning and evening train. The train is a machine but it is also a device of the rulers. It acquires meanings by the way it functions for individuals.

Another metaphoric connection is created by the dance of the bugs in PP and carried in a similar way by other moments of joy. The joy of the moment as Sarbojaya receives the letter with good news extends... but it is also shortlived. As Durga drenches and enjoys the rain, it brings dire consequences. Apu's happy married life is suddenly shattered by Aparna's death... the joy of the happy togetherness was so shortlived. It builds up to the philosophical understanding of the joys of life as shortlived. Man's search for purpose in life and the assertion of the force of love continues despite the quick passing away of the moments of joy.

There are several other details in the design of the work that would suggest connections with the total processes of change, the man-Nature or the man-machine relationship or the economic change reflected in simple articles of everyday use like currency, dress, or food. The forms of entertainment change through the period. As we have seen in the details, the work weaves a close-knit pattern and the changes in the pattern. It rings of truth and authenticity.

Truth and Authenticity in the Trilogy depend upon the care with which every scene is conceived and composed. The possibilities of making the image glossy and glamourous as against the relevant and truthful are open to all filmmakers. Ray, as we have seen, chooses for truth and relevance all the time in the Trilogy, never glamorising any of his images. The rich, complex slice of life is portrayed by the choice of avoiding stereotypes in characters or reduced versions of social norms and value structures or over-simplification in causal connections.

The thematic concern to explore and reveal the predicaments and the conditions of the family and the psychosocial dynamics behind it shows the larger picture. It does not remain a specific story of a specific family, but talks of the larger social process of the period. The quality of truth of an image lies in its capacity to reveal the social reality.

INDEX OF SCENES
(In Rhythm of Three)

PATHER PANCHALI

1/A : PATTERN OF LIVING AT APU'S BIRTH

Guava Stealing Episode

1. Shejobou shouts Durga away. Durga escapes Sarbojaya
2. Durga's world of Indir Auntie and pets
3. Shejobou's verbal lashing of Sarbojaya; Indir leaves after quarrel

Apu is Born

4. Durga sleeps, Harihar paces the floor
5. Mother in pain, attended by Nilmoni's Wife and Shejobou
6. Next morning: neighbour women gather, Indir returns

Dreams of the Family

7. Indir with Apu's cradle, Durga with toybox
8. Harihar and Sarbojaya disagree and agree on family affairs
9. Together they dream of the future; Back to Indir and Apu in cradle

1/B : THE PATTERN AFTER SIX YEARS

Apu Goes to School

10. Morning routine; Apu woken up by Durga
11. Apu made ready for school
12. Apu at school: Gossip; Punishment by teacher

Necklace Stealing Episode

13. Indir Durga and Sarbojaya triangle continues
14. Demands on Harihar increase, demands on children increase
15. Accusation, punishment and reconciliation

Dreams of the Future Persist

16. Indir and children
17. Harihar and Sarbojaya
18. Children go to bed, Indir alone

1/C. STRESS ON THE PATTERN

Chadar Episode and Puja-Jatra

19. Two quarrels: Children's Picnic intercut with Indir-Sarbojaya quarrel
20. Puja-Jatra (Quarrel over Honour)
21. Apu Durga quarrel

Telegraph Poles, Train and Indir's death

22. Children discover telegraph poles, and train

23. Indir's death
24. Mourning

Harihar Leaves
25. Bioscopewallah
26. Sarbojaya as Harihar leaves
27. The children as Harihar leaves

2. STRESS INCREASES AND LEADS TO COLLAPSE

Sarbojaya Holds on
28. Sarbojaya's difficulties and solutions
29. Ranu's marriage
30. Sarbojaya in dire situation

The Happy Letter
31. Harihar's letter brings good news
32. Dance of the bugs
33. Rain.

Durga's Death and Harihar's Decision
34. Durga ill.
35. Storm and death
36. Aftermath of the death and house collapse

3. THE BONDS SNAP

Partings
37. Harihar packs
38. Village elders visit
39. Shejobou and Nilmoni's Wife interact with Sarbojaya.

Apu and Stolen Necklace
40. Apu reaches up the shelf
41. The necklace falls
42. Apu throws it away in the pond

The Family Leaves
43. Family in the bullock cart
44. House and the animals
45. Bullock cart moves on, Sarbojaya breaks down

APARAJITO

Index of Scenes in Rhythm of Three

Pattern of Living in Benares: Physical Features
1. An old man calls pigeons for feeding
2. The Ganga and the varied crowd on the *ghats*
3. Harihar's routine in the morning

Personal and Social Features
4. Sarbojaya and Harihar happily adjust to the new place, neighbours, Apu's new friends
5. Better earning, Apu's play, neighbour's benign gesture
6. Two strangers, Kalicharan and Nandababu, respond to Sarbojaya's presence

The Presiding Deity
7. The temple crowd for Arti
8. Sarbojaya and Apu attend Arti
9. Apu watches in awe

First Signs of Harihar's Illness
10. Festivities

11. Harihar comes home, feeling unwell.
12. Harihar and Sarbojaya talk about shifting to a better house

Tension Mounts

13. Harihar insists on going to the river, faints on his way back.
14. Pandey, a neighbour and others help
15. Sarbojaya defends herself against Nandbabu's ill intentions

Harihar's Death

16. Temple prayers
17. Harihar asks for Ganga Jal, Apu gets it, Harihar breathes his last.
18. Apu helped by elders for funeral rites

Bhabataran's Offer

19. Sarbojaya as a cook
20. Bhabataran offers to take both to Manasapota
21. Sarbojaya declines temporarily

Sarbojaya Tries to Continue

22. Sarbojaya works
23. Apu works, gets a tip
24. Apu spends the tip

Sarbojaya Decides to Take Bhabataran's Offer

25. The landlady asks Sarbojaya to accompany the family to Dewanpur
26. Sarbojaya agrees tentatively
27. Upon watching Apu as a servant, she decides to leave Benaras

Moving out of Benaras

28. Bhabtaran, Sarbojay and Apu on the train out of Benaras
29. The journey, Apu asleep in mother's lap
30. Sarbojaya brightens as the train enters familiar rural scene of Bengal

Apu's Training Starts

31. Sarbojaya settles and sees hope for Apu
32. Bhabataran instructs Apu in performing daily ritual
33. Apu watches children play, runs to the school after his routine

Apu's School Begins

34. Apu pleads with Sarbojaya about attending school
35. She raises the problem of money
36. Apu asks about money, she gives consent

Apu Does Well in School

37. Preparation for inspection
38. The inspector arrives
39. Inspector pleased with Apu's reading skill

Apu's Mind Opens up to the World

40. Apu receives encouragement from the Headmaster
41. Apu agrees to work harder, read more
42. Apu experiments with what he has learned

Apu Matriculates with Good Marks

43. Apu, now grown up, being congratulated for his second rank in the district.
44. Headmaster offers help for higher education in Calcutta
45. Doubts about mother's views

Apu Aspires to go to Calcutta

46. Sarbojaya happy with success but upset about his plan to go away
47. Apu tells her about the scholarship
48. She expresses her concern

Apu and Mother in Conflict

49. Sarbojaya talks about the ancestral profession
50. Apu wants to step out
51. She slaps him

Reconciliation

52. Apu goes out of the house in a huff
53. Pause as Sarbojaya goes in
54. She comes out and gives consent. Apu enthusiastically shows her Calcutta is on the globe

Apu's Departure, Arrival in Calcutta

55. Apu leaves for Calcutta, Sarbojaya left alone
56. Apu on train, lost in the globe, oblivious of the balmseller
57. The train arrives in Calcutta

Apu Settles in Calcutta

58. Apu finds the address of Akhil Babu
59. The agreement, the room and the letter to mother
60. Apu attends college and works in the night shift

Apu Struggles

61. Apu driven out of the classroom for dozing, along with Shibnath
62. They go for a walk, talk about aspirations
63. Apu talks about mother's views

Apu's First Visit

64. Sarbojaya prepares for Apu's arrival. Apu comes and goes for a dip
65. At mealtime she asks about the food he gets
66. At bedtime, she wants him to talk to her, but he sleeps off as she speaks

Apu's Hesitation /Confusion

67. Apu bored in the village: watches a street acrobat, moves away, alone
68. Apu's refusal to stay on and instruction to wake him early.
69. Mother does not wake him, upon waking he leaves in a hurry.

Apu spends one more day

70. Apu at the station
71. The train arrives, Apu does not board
72. Apu comes home, catches with some sleep

Distance between Apu and Mother Grows

73. Apu at exams. The routine of work, studies and friends continues
74. Letter from Sarbojaya pleading him to visit
75. Apu answers in the negative

Sarbojaya Ill and Alone, Apu away, She Succumbs

76. Disappointment of Apu's letter, a neighbourwoman chatters about Apu's marriage; Nirupama finds Sarbojaya ill and alone, Sarbojaya prevents her from writing to Apu
77. Apu at Calcutta, his misjudgement
78. Sarbojaya ill, hallucinates Apu, collapses

Apu Severes Bonds with Ancestral Profession

79. Apu receives letter about mother's illness, rushes home on the train, oblivious of the balmseller
80. Apu rushes home, finds Bhabataran instead and knows; he mourns.
81. Apu and Bhabataran: Bhabataran consoles and advises, Apu declines, Apu leaves Manasapota with mother's belongings, barefoot on his way to the station

APUR SANSAR

Prologue

Apu receives a testimonial from his professor

The Professor praises his writing and advises him to think of writing as a profession. Apu takes his leave as a procession passes by

Apu and His Calcutta Surroundings

1. Rainy morning; Apu asleep; the ink stained chadar, Apu drenches and enjoys the rain
2. Apu and the landlord who demands twenty one rupees that are three months' rent arrears.
3. Apu's namesake neighbour who hands him over a letter delivered to him by mistake

Apu Fails to Find a Job

4. Apu at a primary school. He is rejected because he is overqualified
5. Apu at a pharmaceutical labeling unit. He is repulsed by the working conditions
6. Apu on his way home, frustrated, seeking solace in the publisher's letter and music, avoiding a girl in the next building

Pulu Finds Apu

7. Pulu knocks the door, enters and old friends meet after a long gap
8. Pulu talks about the efforts he took to find his address
9. They decide to go out. Apu promises him a meal of potato and rice some day

Pulu and Apu at the Restaurant

10. They compare notes
11. Pulu inquires about his job and skill of typing, the possibility of a job
12. Pulu aks about the railway job.Apu did not take it because that was against the workers on strike

Pulu and Apu: Invitation to Join in for a Family Marriage

13. Pulu makes the suggestion
14. Apu resists, Pulu gives a tempting description of the place
15. Apu agrees

Pulu and Apu : After the Play

16. Apu recites a poem loudly A policeman calls.They escape shouting about their identitites from the mythological stories
17. Apu refuses the idea of taking a job because he wants to be free to write
18. Apu talks about the novel he has started and an argument over imagination and experience ensues

On the River to Khulna

19. The countryside by the river; Apu plays flute
20. Apu recites a poem
21. Pulu reads Apu's novel and congratulates him

The Arranged Marriage Called off

22. Preparations
23. The arrival of the bridegroom and the fiasco
24. Aparna's mother refuses to let the marriage take place.

Apu Gets Married

25. The crisis in the family: finding another bridegroom
26. Apu approached with a proposal
27. Apu's reservations and consent

Apu and Aparna: Trust and Transparency

28. Apu anxious in the bridal chamber, establishes rapport with Aparna
29. Apu tells Aparna about his condition and checks what she knows and whether she is ready to take a life with him under poor conditions, Aparna agrees
30. Apu relaxed, decides to take her to Calcutta

Apu and Aparna : Confidence and Mutuality

31. Apu and Aparna in the Calcutta room, Aparna sheds tears, Apu introduces her to the neighbours
32. Apu tries to get a servant, Aparna prevents such expense
33. Aparna's prank with the paper bag. At mealtime, Aparna fans when Apu eats, Apu fans sleepily when Aparna eats

Apu and Aparna : Fun and Maturity

34. Aparna delays going to bed by wanting to learn more English
35. Apu and Aparna at the cinema hall

watching a mythological movie.

36. The ride home in horse cart. Talk about separation, dedicating the novel to wife, romance averted tactfully

Aparna's Departure

37. Murari and Aparna in the train compartment
38. Apu and Aparna wordless; the train starts and Aparna breaks into a spate of instructions
39. The train leaves, Apu left alone

Aparna's Letter

40. Apu at work, reminisces about Aparna
41. His colleague notices his happiness
42. Apu reads the letter.

Colleague and Apu

43. Colleague talks about Apu's happiness
44. He talks about his overobedient wife
45. Apu reads the letter on his way home

Murari Brings Bad News

46. As Apu returns from work, he finds Murari waiting at the door
47. Murari falteringly tells about Aparna's death
48. Apu violently hits Murari and collapses

Apu Lost in Grief

49. Apu in bed, lies tearless for a whole day and more
50. Neighbour woman comes in and talks about Aparna's sweet and good nature, possibility of another marriage for Apu, keeps a plate with food on the table.
51. Apu gets up with difficulty, reflected in the mirror.

Apu Writes to Pulu and Leaves Calcutta

52. Apu near the railway tracks, in despair, an engine approaches, he backs
53. A pig hurt by the engine; carried off the tracks by people.
54. Apu writes to Pulu and goes away on a train

Apu on Train

55. Apu at a window, as the train rushes away speedily
56. Aparna's baby in cradle
57. Aparna's mother heaves a sigh and sobs

Apu on Seashore

58. Apu with a beard on the seashore
59. Apu watches the waves
60. The waves wash away the marks on the sand

Apu Consigns the Novel to the Wind

61. Apu wandering aimlessly through a forest.
62. Apu at dawn, goes up a hill, takes out the manuscript
63. He throws the pages to the wind, watches as they scatter and are taken away by the wind

Kajal, Apu's Son, Now Six

64. Kajal with a mask and sling indulging in unruly mischief, scolded, branded as taking to stealing; watched by Pulu
65. Pulu back from the stay abroad, hears about Apu's total neglect of the child
66. Pulu takes Apu's address from his uncle

Pulu Reminds Apu of His Responsibility

67. Pulu finds Apu near a ropeway of a coal mine.
68. Pulu comes to know about the novel.
69. He reminds Apu of his duty towards his son and leaves. Apu desolate.

Apu Comes to See Kajal

70. Apu at the house in Khulna; Father-in-law does not recognise him
71. Kajal asleep; Apu waits. Memories well up.
72. Upon waking he runs away, Apu calls after him

Apu Fails to Connect with Kajal

73. Uncle watches the two, Apu runs to the gate and tells Kajal who he is
74. Uncle by Apu's side, Kajal hurls a stone at Apu.
75. Uncle calls Kajal, raises his stick to punish, Apu holds his hand back.

Kajal Watches but Runs away; Kajal Rejects Apu

76. Apu brings a toy engine.
77. Kajal looks at him and throws back the toy at him vehemently.
78. In bed, Apu tries to win him by stories, but gets no response

Kajal Trusts Apu

79. Apu gets ready to leave without his son, hands over Aparna's jewellery. Uncle urges him to take the son away by force.
80. Kajal watches Apu as he starts to leave. Apu tries again to connect. Kajal checks if he would take him to his father, and whether the father would be cross with him.
81. When Apu answers in the affirmative, and grandfather comes looking for him, Kajal decides to trust Apu as a friend and runs towards him. Perched on Apu's shoulders, Kajal starts the journey to his father in Calcutta.

Interconnections of Design

This appendix indicates how elements repeat elsewhere with similarity, contrast, balance and resolution to create the warp and woof of the design. The entries here are by no means exhaustive. More relationships can be, and should be found. In fact, this listing should stimulate one to discover more and more new relationships.

PATHER PANCHALI
HARIHAR'S PATTERN OF LIVING AT APU'S BIRTH

Guava stealing episode

1. Shejobou's courtyard Shejobou – Durga – Sarbojaya triangle	Repeat in the necklace stealing accusation (PP 15), with variation. Durga is corrected here and punished in PP 15.
Shejobou – Sarbojaya – Nilmoni's Wife triangle	Repeats in PP 5. In both cases the visual composition indicates the difference in the relationships. Both triangularities resolve in PP 39 when Shejobou sheds opposition, brings the gift of fruit and and displays a sense of belonging.
Shejobou – neighbour woman – Mother/Durga as community relations	In PP 15 Shejobou accuses both mother and daughter as thieves.
Shejobou's courtyard as a location	repeats in PP 14, 20, and 29. The guava stealing episode connects with AS64 where Apu's son Kajal plays a prank and is admonished by community members. Concern for correction of child in guava stealing scene is contrasted with threats and punishment to Kajal in AS 64.
2.Durga's world composed of the very old Indir, and pet kitten.)	Connects with her bond with Indir (PP 3, 6, 7, 13, 16, 23 and 24). The circular shape of this world of innocence and security gets emphasized in PP 3, 6 and 7. Animals as pets appear elsewhere (PP 14 and 15). Animals in close relations with humans in the environment appear in many scenes.

3.Sarbojaya's house	
Sarbojaya-Durga –Indir as a triangular relationship	Repeats in PP 6 in a minor manner and sharply in PP 13. Repeats in PP 15 with a subtle shade.
Durga is put to learn household chores like sweeping the courtyard	Durga's upbringing repeats in various forms in PP 11, 14, 19, and 28.
	Durga's upbringing becomes a cause of insult in personal attack (PP 15).
Sarbojaya's house is the central location in the film, and part of it collapses in PP 35	As a basic necessity for survival with dignity, the house and its maintenance becomes progressively more difficult. It connects with other dwellings : the rented house in Benaras they wanted to shift from (APJT 12) and the terrace room in AS1,where the landlord poses ultimatum to Apu for rent appears.

Apu is Born

4.Durga sleeps, Harihar paces the floor	In contrast Apu sleeps when Durga dies. Harihar is away.
Durga's toybox is seen by her bedside	The toybox appears with variations in PP 7, 15, 21.
5.Mother in pain, attended by Nilmoni's Wife and Shejobou	The trio now is seen as women who share norm of mutual help. Contrast to PP 1 situation. It is repeated in PP 39 with similarity, Shejobou a little distant and Nilmoni's Wife sympathetic and friendly.
6.Next morning. neighbour women gather, Indir returns	Togetherness tends to form a circular shape. Neighbours gather around the centre, in this case, newborn Apu.
	The circularity emphasized by coming together. Neighbour women in PP 1, 15, 28.
	Across the Trilogy, sympathetic neighbour women appear as Pandey's Wife, APJT 4 and in AS 31, 50 with variations.
Indir accepted in family fold	Durga-Indir bond carried through.
	In PP 7, Indir seen as helping in looking after infant Apu.
	By contrast, Indir rejected in PP 19 and 23.

Apu as the centre	As he is helped in preparation for going to school (PP 11).
	Scenes of violence done in terms of Apu's reaction (PP 11 and PP 14).
	Bandplayers at the time of Ranu's marriage. Apu emerges from the crowd, getting at the centre (PP 29).

Dreams of the Family

7.Indir rocks Apu's cradle, Durga with her toybox	Apu and Indir together have similarity too (PP 6) where Durga and Indir share their toothless quality
	Durga's counting skill comes in again in PP 19 when she counts the number of days to go for Ranu's marriage.
8.Harihar and Sarbojaya talk about the house repairs, Durga's marriage, Apu's education	The three major concerns of the family are worked through in events in PP. The house deteriorates (PP 28), part of it collapses (PP 35). It is abandoned (PP 44). Durga's marriage is talked about but her death ends it all (PP 35). The upbringing of the girl child worked in terms of Ranu (PP 29). Across the Trilogy In APJT 76 Apu's marriage is talked about and in AS 27 as Aparna gets married to Apu by chance.
	The girls were trained to be like Aparna, seen in AS 19 to 39.
	Apu's education is seen gradually as he learns to read and write in PP, it becomes a central concern in APJT and in AS the half educated unemployed status of Apu is similar to Harihar's traditional training in priesthood rather than knowledge of scholarly erudition.
Sarbojaya's fears	The fears come true as the dreams collapse one by one Durga's death (PP 32). House collapse (PP 32) and. Apu has to discontinue his education, Prologue, AS.
9.The family together, Indir and finally Apu in the frame	Repeats in decimation in PP 43, 45 in APJT 28.
	With variation in AS in AS 19 – 39
	Another variation in AS 81.

THE PATTERN AFTER SIX YEARS
Apu Goes to School

10.Daily morning routine	Repetition with variation of PP 1
	Morning routines appear in APJT and AS in the opening sequences.
11.Apu prepared for school	Contrast Apu cleaning teeth, combing hair, going out on path after Durga's death (PP 35)
	Sarbojaya's adoration of Apu as he tells her what he learns (APJT 42) and where Calcutta is on the globe model (APJT 54).
Apu at the centre of attention of the womenfolk	Note the circular composition of Apu's world of innocence and security.
	In APJT Apu grows independent and actively insists on going to school (APJT 33).
	Contrasts with Kajal with the insecurity of parental absence (AS 64).
12.Apu at school: Gossip and punishment	Contrasts with Kajal with the insecurity of parental absence (AS 64).
Writing and recitation:	Seen on wall of the house (PP 14) .
	Apu reads the address on the letter (PP 32). Reading skill admired in (APJT 39).
Writing and recitation:	Apu's writing admired (AS Prologue & 21).
The adults gossip:	the community celebration at Puja time (PP 20). the community gathering at Ranu's marriage (PP 29). Concern of community about Harihar's leaving (PP 38). Community participation (APJT 18) for Indir's funeral.
Punishment as exposure to violence	Durga is punished (PP 15). Apu is turned out of the class (APJT 61).

Necklace stealing sequence

13.Indir Durga and Sarbojaya triangle continues	Sharp criticism by Sarbojaya, a repetition of PP 3.
	Durga –Indir bond repeated here (PP 2, 6, 12).
Durga's growth	Repeats in PP 14, 19, 23, 28, 33.
14. Demands on Harihar increase, Indir's torn Chadar	The hole as a circular motif seen earlier in PP 2 repeats with variations in PP 11, 23, 42 and AS 31. The chadar repeats in PP 19.

. demands by children increase Chinibas, the sweetseller appears	Apu does not get something to eat, Durga improvises sour pickle . Apu does not get pice to buy sweets; They follow Chinibas to Shejobou's house. Ranu arranges a sweet for Durga, who also wants to handle bead necklace.
The evening lamp at the Tulsi plant	connects with the lamp Sarbojaya carries in PP 28 & 35 carrying overtones of meaning.
Harihar's writing of a horoscope is part of his ancestral profession	Apu abandons by the end of APJT 81.
Apu's writing on slate	Connects with the concern for his education.
The train whistle is heard and the children discuss	They will go on an adventure (PP 22). The train motif runs through the Trilogy.
Ranu's marriage is talked about	It will be worked out in PP 29.
Durga wants her hair done in four braids	Durga's hair are dry and cannot be made in four braids. In contrast, Bini, Nilmoni's daughter will have it (PP 36).
15.accusation, punishment and reconciliation	This unit is a high intensity triangle placed between two units of parental care.
Apu being fed by mother. He keeps on playing with bow and arrow	Contrast with absence of mother for Kajal (AS 64).
The door bangs open and Shejobou comes in offensively	The door bang repeats in storm (PP 35).
Sarbojaya insulted about her daughter being trained as a thief.	She feels insulted by Indir begging for a chadar from an outsider (PP 19).
Shejobou shouts accusations for others to hear	repeat from PP 1.
Durga's punishment shown with of Apu's reaction	When drum beat background music repeats on Apu as he throws the stolen bead necklace in the pond to maintain the secret of the dead sister, it appears that Apu is all over being punished again for the sister's act (PP 41 & 42).
Sarbojaya collapses in exhaustion	Repeats in APJT 15 with high emotional intensity of defending herself.

Indir and Apu try to behave to alleviate mother's rage and sorrow	Contrast in APJT 75 when Apu has moved away from mother.
Mother reconciles with Durga	Repeats in APJT 54.

Dreams of the Future Persist

16.Indir and children A form of entertainment	A horror story for children's entertainment. Repeats in PP 19, 20, 25, 29, 33 in the forms of picnic, Jatra, Bioscope, and the rain itself. In APJT 7-9, the temple arti has an element of spectacle, in APJT 10 the crackers and lamps offer the festive spirit, in APJT 17 Apu watches a body building exercise, in APJT 42 learning is fun for Apu, in APJT 67 Apu is bored by the acrobat. In AS 16 Apu goes for a play, takes Aparna to a movie (AS 36). Kajal wears a mask and has a sling to aim at birds (AS 64). Anticipates the fear inspired in Sarbojaya (PP 17).
17.Harihar and Sarbojaya	The contrast continues from PP 3 Harihar has his optimism and Sarbojaya senses danger.
	Both optimistic in APJT 12 as a contrast.
Harihar at meal as Sarbojaya fans	Contrast with Apu fanning when Aparna eats AS 32.
18. Children go to bed. Durga tells a lie	The lie is given away in PP 41. The tension resolved by Apu's moral act (PP 42).
Harihar sleeps as Sarbojaya talks of her dreams	Similarity with (APJT 66), Apu sleeps as she talks of her worries.
Indir's song	played on an instrument in PP 3 &19, sung here by her. It is repeated in her voice over her funeral (PP 23).

Stress on the Pattern
Chadar – Puja Jatra

19. Children's Picnic intercut with Indir Sarbojaya quarrel	The contrast between children's world and the quarrels over responsibility, and the adult world where the quarrel (about the new chadar) between Indir and Sarbojaya over norm and honour of the provider of the house take a decisive turn. The little quarrel is resolved by Ranu acting in a mature manner, links with bringing up the girl child.

Ranu's marriage as a topic of conversation	Durga and Ranu talk about the number of days remaining before her marriage Repeat fr[illegible] PP 14 where the preliminaries are discussed by Durga and mother. Indir seeks shelter in Raju's house (contrast with PP 22).
20.Puja-Jatra (Quarrel over Honour)	The drummers in Shejobou's courtyard: work out from PP 12.
Durga idol	connects with Vishwanath idol in the Temple (APJT 7-9).
Children get new clothes:	Part of the pattern of buying necessities.Link with morning routines (PP 1-3), (PP 10) and yearly preserves (PP 28) .
Durga, along with other children gets a sweet from Shejobou.	Contrast with Shejobou's reaction to Durga's presence when she was buying sweets from Chinibas (PP 14).
The Jatra performance deals with the issue of honour, Serpent king vs. a human being.	The quarrel between Sarbojaya and Indir is about honour (PP 19).
21. Apu Durga quarrel	This is over pilfering tinsel from Durga's toybox. More playful, but the issues of rights and responsibility are built in, as in the two preceding quarrels.
Durga's grimace	Connects with her putting her tongue out in the night scene when Sarbojaya makes her hair, with the same gesture in the rain sequence (PP 33) and for following the doctor's instructions as he examines her when she falls ill (PP 34).

Telegraph Poles, Train intercut with Sarbojaya's last denial of shelter to Indir and Indir's death

22.Children discover Telegraph poles, and train	
Apu and Durga run across fields, far off from the house as a cloud passes over the landscape	This will be followed quickly by the smoke covering the sky.
Natural background for the fiction of the Trilogy.	The scenes of expanse of fields, (as seen here), River (APJT opening, AS 19) and the forest (AS 61-63). Human life has this backdrop of plentiful Nature during the period of the fiction.
Apu gets confused in the patch of tall Kaansh grass	Durga too does not know. Confusion with greater intensity repeated in APJT 67-69 when he returns from the station, with much greater intensity in AS 25-28 when he is anxious about Aparna's response to the marriage.

Small Apu and big train as he watches it	The sense of awe repeats in APJT 7-9 at the Vishwanath temple : Aparna's death as a massive blow in AS 46-48. In all the cases the forces are beyond his comprehension and control.
Indir asks for shelter, Sarbojaya denies	The quarrel over norm, actions and honour has spiraled to this end. The intensity is high with Indir's last effort at reconciliation. Repeat of Indir trying to soothe Sarbojaya when she has a coughing fit (PP 19) and earlier, when she is angry and sorry (PP 15).
Indir waters the plant	A repetition of her earlier action in PP 1.
23. Indir's death Children discover Indir in her last moments	She was a part of their world, particularly Durga's (PP 4, 7, 9, 13, 15…).
Indir's pot tumbles down into the pond	Part of Indir's character : She uses it (PP 3), carries it (PP 3), waters plant with leftover water (PP 21) A parallel to Indir's insignificance and the battered quality of her life.
Indir dies in loneliness	Indir carried by the pallbearers visually with the song in her own voice on the sound track create a design of irony.
24.Mourning The children sit on Indir's verandah, now without Indir	Reminder of PP 3 when she ate and Durga sat by Reminder of rocking Apu in the cradle, Reminder of the horror story she told
Harihar comes from the pond with his pot, passes Sarbojaya Harihar says nothing Sarbojaya stands alone	Repeat in the last scene (PP 36) where Sarbojaya breaks down and Harihar also breaks down and says nothing.

Harihar leaves

25.Bioscopewallah The peep box show of distant places.	Another outsider coming to the village, like the band players (PP 29), baul mendicant (PP 28), Chinibas (PP 14 & 34) and the drummers and Jatra players (PP 20).
26. Sarbojaya as Harihar leaves with very few words spoken	Repeats in AS 37-39 as Aparna goes away. The difference and similarity of their prayers as he folds his hands to the Ganesh idol and she to the Omnipresent as he leaves.
27.Harihar and children as he leaves	
Apu gets a coin to watch the bioscope show	Contrast with Chinibas scene in PP 14 where Apu asks but does not get money.

Harihar sees Durga for the last time.	Overtonal resonance with Sarbojaya seeing Apu off (APJT 55). With Apu seeing off Aparna (AS 39). Indir's last look at the house (PP 22).

PP2: Stress Mounts, Collapse
Sarbojaya Holds on

28.Sarbojaya's difficulties and solutions: Spending a pice for making a sweet for Apu. The first letter with disappointing news	First element of routine of making yearly preserves Reminder of the contrast of her insistence that children should not buy sweets from Chinibas. (PP 14). Contrast with the second letter with happy news.
Baul mendicant at the door	Threat to the repute of the house when she has very little grain in the house.
Durga saves the situation	Aspect of her growth.
In the night she takes out the costly utensils for selling	Repeat of a wordless scene (PP 24, 45).
29.Ranu's marriage	Placed between two scenes of dire conditions for survival in Sarbojaya's house.
	Done in terms of Apu in the courtyard crowd around the bandplayers,
	Sarbojaya in the kitchen with other village women helping in the kitchen for the marriage feast,
	Durga, the friend and dramatic opposite of Ranu as Ranu's bridal décor is completed and the marriage ritual is completed.
	Contrast with Apu's marriage in AS 27.
The community and the custom emphasised here	Apu emphasizes individuality in AS.
Ranu's consent not an issue	Apu wants to make sure about Aparna's consent.
30.Sarbojaya in dire situation Nilmoni's Wife leaves a coin	At the end of her resources, Sarbojaya has come to survive on near-charity from Nilmoni's Wife.

The Happy Letter

31.Harihar's letter brings good news Apu's progress in reading as he holds the letter and reads Sarbojaya's name	Repeat of Apu's 'good' behaviour to please mother when she is upset (PP 15). Repeat in APJT 39 where he is appreciated.
Sarbojaya's face lightens up	Contrast with the darkening in PP 28.
The good news brings relaxation after a long time	Immediate contrast with the previous scene of tension over no food in the house.
The ripples of her joy spread into the next unit.	Dissolve over Sarbojaya's smile and the ripples on the surface of water.
32.Dance of the bugs Sheer joy of visual beauty. The sense of freedom from worries and enjoyment. The bugs on the surface of the pond using their space freely, fully.	A moment of Director's privilege. Variation in design/contrast in mood (APJT 78) when the fireflies dance before Sarbojaya's eyes Another variation (AS 63) as the pages of Apu's manuscript scatter in wilderness.
The reflection of a twig of a plant	Repeat of the reflection of the line of Chinibas, Durga, Apu and the dog in a procession to Shejobou's house (PP 14).
Friendly play between a cat and a dog	benign feelings around Sarbojaya: an overtone of her moment of joy.
33. Rain Durga grooms herself with Kajal and Bindi	Another aspect of her growth. Similarity with Apu trying to put a moustache and pretending to be 'grown up' in PP 20. Aparna puts on sindoor and bindi when getting ready to receive Apu in the evening (AS 11).
Durga performs a brat	Her lingering childhood as she hurries through the rite to run out in the rain.
The first raindrop on a bald man's head, he senses and opens the umbrella by a reflex	Umbrellas in several scenes: (PP 26) Harihar, Apu after Durga's death (PP 36). In APJT 2 big umbrellas on the Ganga ghats.
The door bangs Sarbojaya wakes up and calls Durga who has already run away	In APJT 78 she hallucinates Apu's call and he does not come. Apu in APJT 79 calls for mother and she is no more.

Durga and Apu in rain Both drench in the rain Apu calls Durga Durga's grimace	Contrast with adults rushing for shelter in the previous scene Durga continues to enjoy rain. Repeat the grimace as a part of the children's world (PP 21) Repeat with variation in the next scene (PP 34)
Durga's protective gesture for Apu	Repeat of Durga escorting Apu to school (PP 11) Variation in PP 35 where mother tries to protect Durga from the stormy wind
Durga and Apu recite for the rain to go away	Recitations : School dictation (PP12). Apu reading from the book after Durga's punishment (PP 15). Durga's hurried recitation of the brat ritual in the previous scene (PP 32). Apu's reading at the school inspection in APJT 39. Apu's recitations in AS16 & 19.
Durga sneezes	Reference to her susceptibility in PP 13 where mother checks her fever.

Durga's death and Harihar's decision

34.Durga ill Helping neighbours Nilmoni and Nilmoni's Wife	Repeat from PP 5 & 6 at the time of Apu's birth. From PP 29 at the time of Ranu's marriage. In APJT 14 when Harihar is ill. In AS 50 when Apu is lost in grief.
The village doctor examines Durga, advises cold fomentation and sago	A doctor is called in by Pandey in APJT 50 to examine Harihar.
Durga had missed the train	Durga's simple desires that are denied by life (PP 1) fruit she would like to eat (PP 14) sweet and threading the beads. Contrast with desires satisfied like getting the fruit by pilfering, getting the pice from Harihar to watch the bioscope show (PP 27), getting the new clothes (PP 19).
Chinibas passes by, Durga in high fever turned away	Contrast with Durga licking her lips when Chinibas announces the delicacies PP 14.
35.Storm and death Apu asleep	Reversal of PP 4.

The rising wind and rain The curtain gives way	Similarity with Apu's room having a torn curtain (AS 1) . Contrast with the new curtain that Aparna has put (AS 31).
The Ganesh idol shakes	Contrast to Harihar's faith when he prayed before leaving.
The door comes to the breaking point, Sarbojaya pushes a heavy trunk to prevent its collapse	Reminder of Sarbojaya's all out effort to save the situation in PP 28.
36. Aftermath Apu knocks Nilmoni's door	The sturdy bolt as a contrast to Sarbojaya's door, also in PP 28. Repeat of the door of Shejobou's house with a heraldic lion (PP 1)
The devastation of the house, the dead frog noticeable.	Animals live and die as parts of nature, just like human beings. Details of animals through the films done in the spreadout.
Sarbojaya entirely drained of energy with dead Durga in her lap	Contrast with her strength (PP 15), (PP 18) and later, in (APJT 15). Similar but high in intensity to her exhaustion in PP 15.
Wordless sympathy from Nilmoni's Wife	Similar in wordlessness and different in feelings from PP 1 when she casts a disapproving glance at Shejobou's terrace.
Life goes on	Repeat morning routine of drawing water from the well, Apu grooming himself. Reminders of Durga in her absence and the pain of it.
Apu going out, taking care to carry an umbrella	A very different use of the umbrella for the expressive function Umbrella as an object is repeated, but here for indicating the change in Apu
Bini comes with vegetables, Sarbojaya distracted	Another aspect of neighbours' help Bini as reminder of Durga and her hair done in four braids as Durga had wanted
Harihar returns Calls, shows things, Sari for Durga Sarbojaya breaks down, The mother's wail music	The contrast in the expression of grief over the loss of one's child. Physical contact in sympathy and sharing
Harihar lies awake and decides, the train whistle	The train whistle on Sarbojaya's face when she decides in APJT to leave Benaras (APJT 27) Repeat in AS 51

PP3:Bonds Snapped

Partings

37.Harihar packs	The pages he leafs through resemble the paper on which the titles of the film appear.
38.Village elders visit Harihar talks about the help he was sure to get from them but the total frustration of his aspirations	The community elders question his decision, but know they are ineffective. Similar to Indir making inquiries during the accusation of Durga and no one pays any heed. Contrast with his optimism even in difficult times.
39.Shejobou and Nilmoni's Wife interact with Sarbojaya	The triangularity resolved here as Shejobou brings a gift of a basketful of mangoes and talks about the need for change and how it makes you meanminded when you are stagnant in one place.
Apu and stolen Necklace	
40.Apu reaches up the shelf	Similar to Apu getting the oil in PP 13.
41. The necklace falls, Drums on the sound track	A spider crawls across, part of the animal world. Reminder of the punishment (PP 15) and Apu's shock and anxiety.
42. Apu throws it away The pond surface covered with moss parts as the necklace drops in it, but leaves an uneven circular tear like gap.	Apu's growth after Durga's death (PP 36), Apu's moral act in keeping the dead sister's ugly secret. Reminder of Indir's torn chadar.
Family leaves	
43.Family in the bullock cart	The final snapping of the bond. Indir's bond snapped (PP 19 & 20). Community bonds snapped in the scene with Village elders (PP 37).
44. House and the animals; the dog left behind and a serpent enters the house, now empty and slithers across the verandah	Reminder of human beings using the path. Snake and a house as culturally loaded image. The range of animals spread out from the predators to the prey, the domesticated ones and the wild ones.
45. Bullock cart moves, Sarbojaya breaks down	The family has left a pattern of living and will try a new one. This will repeat with the Benares pattern, with the Manasapota pattern in Aparajito and with Apu's pattern of togetherness in Apur Sansar.

APARAJITO

Now onwards, the larger units will be taken up for design connections. The details that connect across the Trilogy have already been indicated with respect to Pather Panchali.
Internal connections with APJT will be pointed out, as also the elements from APJT which link with AS.

APJT 1:Pattern of Living in Benares

Physical Features

1.Call of an old man calling pigeons for feeding	Contrast with flock of pigeons which flies away when Harihar dies (APJT17)
2.The Ganga and the crowd on the ghats	The great river is the large backdrop for physical environment of Benaras, as also the centre of socio-cultural life. This place is different from Nishchindipur in terms of crowds and composition of population.
3. Harihar's morning routine.	As a Brahmin, bath in the river is a daily sacred act, all the more essential for a Brahmin Kathawachak on the ghats. The roadside deities under trees are a new element from the ghat location. The practice of serving each with holy water reminds of Indir watering plants in Harihar's courtyard.

Personal and Social Features

4.Sarbojaya and Harihar happily adjust to the new place and new neighbours; Apu's new friends	These are aspects of settling in a new place with basically the same relationships: neighbours, friends for Apu and more male company for Harihar.
The house	Very different layout. Tap water supply is a great convenience. There is a major inconvenience like the lack of privacy for Sarbojaya.
5.Better earning	Working out of Sarbojaya's suggestion in PP 17.
Apu's play,	The shape of the children's world is different, but the spirit persists. Apu has found friends and playmates.
Neighbour's gestures	Pandey's family invites Sarbojaya to join them in the morning routine of Ganga bath. Nandababu gifts a calendar.
6.Two strangers, Kalicharan and Nandababu, respond to Sarbojaya's presence	A new experience of being regarded as a woman. Receives appreciation for making good tea. Kalicharan's desire to get married is triggered by her presence. Nandababu makes an improper advance at a later point when she is vulnerable (APJT 15).

The Presiding Deity

7.The temple crowd at Aarti	Vishwanath temple as the central prosperous institution, wielding influence on the devotees.
8. Sarbojaya and Apu attend Arti	The laying of the Benaras pattern culminates in this scene.
9.Apu watches in awe	Apu is surrounded by the influence of the ancestral profession.
	Between the two scenes of Arti, the pattern is strained and collapses (APJT16).

The Strain and Collapse
First Signs of Harihar's Illness

10. Festivities	Similarity with Puja Jatra in PP. More individual celebrations. Mention of Ramlila.
11. Harihar comes home, feeling unwell	Harihar tries to handle the difficulty with a traditional medicine.
12.Harihar and Sarbojaya talk about shifting to a better house	The optimism comes up, parallel to the dreams of the family in PP.
	The first signs of strain do not affect the spirit as Apu too shows his progress in learning English from a friend.

Tension Mounts

13.Harihar insists on going to the river, faints on his way back	Repetition of Harihar's tendency to disregard danger
14 Pandey, a neighbour and others help	Later, Nirupama a neighbour would help Sarbojaya when Apu is away (APJT 61-78)
15.Sarbojaya defends herself against Nandababu's improper advance.	Repetition of Sarbojaya's strength.
	Sarbojaya faces two kinds of threats – Harihar's health and her own safety.

Harihar's Death

16.Temple prayers	Ritual repetition, force of believers, connects two kinds of threats to Sarbojaya, one preceding the ritual and the other following it.

17.Harihar asks for Ganga Jal, Apu gets it, Harihar breathes his last. A flock of birds flies away	Sarbojaya's fears fully worked out. The reverse of the opening scene where the flock had landed. Apu wonders at the strength of the body builder.Repetition of his response in APJT 5.
18.Apu helped by elders for preparation of funeral rites	Community help persists in the relatively strange place.
	Harihar's death in a holy place, with the son giving Ganga Jal and performing last rites is treated differently from other deaths. Apu's participation in the funeral at the tender age is part of the customary religious practice. Indir and Durga we see on the screen, later on Sarbojaya and Aparna die but their deaths are done in terms of Apu. Here, Apu does not quite comprehend the deaths he sees, but is hit hard by the other two.

Sarbojaya Decides to Leave Benaras
Bhabtaran's Offer

19. Sarbojaya as a cook	Design of her overcoming the difficulties of living
20. Bhabataran offers to take both to Manasapota	Help from the family member, possibility of continuing the family profession
21. Sarbojaya declines temporarily	Sarbojaya tries to hold on to the bigger place.
	Life goes on, after Harihar's death too. A new pattern has to be built.

Sarbojaya Tries to Continue

22. Sarbojaya works	Reminder of her cooking mentioned earlier, and later by Apu (APJT 65)
23. Apu works, gets a tip	Apu in a very different role than what the dreams of the family envisaged. A contrast of the dream.
24. Apu spends the tip	Apu's moment of benign joy when he has to be alone.
	This is survival, but not with the dignity that the family was looking for.

Sarbojaya Decides to take Bhabataran's Offer

25. The landlady asks Sarbojaya to accompany the family to Devanpur	Contrast of Sarbojaya as a widow, from the other widows who attended Harihar's katha (APJT 5)
26.Sarbojaya agrees	
27.Upon watching Apu as a servant, she decides to leave Benaras	The point of decision with the train whistle.

	Sarbojaya not drawn in by the approval she finds. Her concern over Apu's future takes her away from this position. Sarbojaya has to hold on in the interest of Apu's future after Harihar's death. There was Shejobou who became a widow in PP 14 supported by the rich family. In Apur Sansar, in a social contrast, Apu loses his wife. The contrast works in terms of social expectations, personal reactions and purposes in living

Moving Out of Benaras

28.Bhabtaran, Sarbojay and Apu on the train out of Benaras	The train moves in the opposite direction to the entry in Benaras in the beginning.
29. The journey, Apu asleep in mother's lap	When the decimated family left ancestral village, it was the bullock cart. When the family decimated further, leaves the Benaras location, it leaves on the train and returns to the village. Later on when Apu abandons Manasapota and the ancestral profession, he leaves barefoot along the path to the railway station. (APJT 81).
30. Sarbojaya brightens as the train enters familiar rural scene of Bengal	The PP theme music repeated here. Sarbojaya's comfort with the familiar scene seen on her face.

Apu's Training Starts

31. Sarbojaya settles and sees hope for Apu	Similar rural dwelling.
32.Bhabtaran instructs Apu in performing daily ritual	Traditional method of instruction in the family profession.
33.Apu watches children play, runs to the school after his routine	Apu is not a natural member of this group. Contrast from his Nishchindipur group.
	Ever since the Benaras days, Apu has been watching a wider, different world, not accessed by Sarbojaya.

Apu's School Begins

34.Apu pleads with Sarbojaya about attending school	Sarbojaya as a sensitive mother.
35.She raises the problem of money	Sarbojaya's investing in Apu's future leads to the distancing. The distancing between mother and son begins from this point in a subtle way
36. Apu asks about money and she gives cosent	Sarbojaya's concern for Apu's education as in APJT 27 where she decides to leave Benaras.

Apu does well in School, Six Years Pass

37.Preparation for inspection	The system of British education with its formal institutional character.
38.The inspector arrives	The new roles taken up by Indian people, new kinds of jobs.
39. Inspector pleased with Apu's reading skill	Apu gives a good account of himself and the school. Apu's recitation brings out the emotional bond the inspector has with the country. The parallel is seen in AS 13-14 where Apu talks about not taking up the railway job because they were substituting striking workmen. . Repetition in another instance: The boatman in AS responding to Apu's recitation (AS 19)
	The formal aspect emphasised in the dress code, in the process of inspection and the importance given to students showing good progress. This is very different from the school in AS where Apu goes to look for a job (AS4). The Inspector dressed in a three piece suit and a solar hat is at one end of the British influence on the mode of dress. The variations are: The school Headmaster who wears a dhoti, coat and shoes and socks, The attendant who wears a uniform, college students who wear dhotis and shirts, and Prosanna the Nischindipur school teacher who wears a dhoti only. Eventually Apu too would wear shirts and shoes.

Apu's Interest in the New World

40.Apu receives encouragement from the Headmaster	Apu grows with the encouragement received from the personal interest taken by the Head Master, contrasted with the impersonal treatment in the college
41.Apu agrees to work harder, read more	Apu's method of growing into the larger world : Reading and experimenting, seeing for himself
42.Apu experiments with what he has learned	The joy of discovery similar to the joy of adventure when he saw the train Apu's interest in dressing up: The princely crown (PP24) and the African tribesman here.

Six Years Pass

Apu Matriculates with good marks

43.Apu, now grown up, being congratulated for his second rank in the district.	Appreciation of Apu's achievement. Repeat with the publisher's letter of acceptance of his writing (AS 3) and Pulu congratulating him for his writing (AS 19)

44.Headmaster offers help for higher education in Calcutta	New source of help.
45.Doubts about mother's views	Apu distanced from mother as he thinks of personal growth.
	Education has worked as an alienating influence.

Tension and Reconciliation

Apu Aspires to go to Calcutta

46.Sarbojaya happy with success but upset about his plan to go away	The viewpoints of mother and son in direct opposition, it is a threat for Sarbojaya and an opportunity for Apu.
47.Apu tells her about the scholarship	The escalation of the opposition to the point where she slaps Apu.
48.She expresses her concern	

Apu and Mother in Conflict

49.Sarbojaya talks about the ancestral profession	
50. Apu wants to step out	Here, Apu touches her sense of pride in the ancestral profession by not wanting to remain a priest for the whole of his life.
51. She slaps him	The impasse of the argument.

Reconciliation

52. Apu goes out of the house in a huff	Apu's growth and assertion.
53. Pause as Sarbojaya goes in	Visual composition shows the model of the globe in the light of a kerosene lamp.
54. She comes out and gives consent. Apu shows globe	Repetition of Sarbojaya's adoration.
	The whole section is a repeat from PP 15 where Durga was punished by mother.There the issue was her parenting a thief, here it is the sense of honour in the family profession.

Apu as a Struggling Student

Apu's Departure, Arrival in Calcutta

55. Apu leaves for Calcutta, Sarbojaya left alone	After reconciliation, the physical distancing is managed efficiently by both.
56.Apu on train, lost in the globe, oblivious of the balmseller	The balmseller will be repeated APJT 79. The kind of bottle he sells will be repeated in the labeling unit that Apu goes to, looking for a job in AS 5.
57.The train arrives in Calcutta	The tracks and the joints and the complexity of the system, part of the train as a binding motif. The railways play a greater role and Apu travels between the city and Manasapota more frequently.
	The basic difference in the social context established from the very first scene where Apu is one in the crowd. The social significance he has enjoyed so far dwindles as he joins the city life.

Apu Settles in Calcutta

58.Apu finds the address of Akhil Babu	From the railway station through the system of roads and transport, the physical features of the city are introduced. Apu's lone efforts to fulfill his ambitions have begun. In AS 4 Pulu finds his address after great difficulty
59. The agreement, the room and the letter to mother	The electric light will be repeated in AS 2 as he interacts with the landlord. In Benaras it was the tap water supply, here it is the supply of electricity for domestic use
60. Apu attends college and works in the night shift	New urban pattern for a struggling student, earn and learn.

Apu Struggles

61.Apu driven out of the classroom for dozing, along with Shibnath	Contrast with the sympathy shown by the school master.
62.They go for a walk, talk about aspirations	New friends to share problems
63. Apu talks about mother's views	The distance between mother and Apu is growing even in terms of basic concepts like distance and time. she recedes further in APJT 73 where Apu sends money instead of going for a visit. Going abroad mentioned here repeats in AS 68 when he cannot face the responsibility of his son.

	Just as Harihar struggled to maintain the traditional pattern, Apu struggles for the preparation for a take off in the modern world where education is the key.

Apu Distances From Mother

Apu's First Visit

64. Sarbojaya prepares for Apu's arrival. Apu comes and goes for a dip	Food and discussion: Reminders of Harihar Sarbojaya interaction.
65.At bedtime, she wants him to talk to her, but he sleeps off as she speaks	Sarbojaya's loneliness deepened by separation-here, by sleep (PP 18).
	Mother's joy gets mellowed as he seems so distant.

Apu's Hesitation/Confusion

66.Apu bored in the village	The acrobat fails to entertain Apu, contrast with Jatra. The acrobat chant is perhaps the same as what Apu is out to do: Show your excellence to the world. But he has so distanced himself from the ideas of doing well that tradition would have him that he gets bored. This 'show' does not entertain him anymore.
67.Apu's refusal to stay on and instruction to wake him early	Higher intensity of distancing.
68. Mother does not wake him, upon waking he leaves in a hurry	Helplessness and again being left alone for Sarbojaya.

Apu spends one more day

69.Apu at the station	Visual symmetry of Apu by a pole on the station, Sarbojaya by a pole supporting the verandah.
70.The train arrives, Apu does not board	More details of the railway system.
71.Apu comes home, catches with some sleep	A kind of satisfaction for Sarbojaya, contrasted with her agony at his leaving in a hurry in somewhat irritated mood.
	Lingering childhood and the grown up adolescence together. Reminder of Durga's similar condition in the rain sequence (PP 32-33).

Apu Abandons Ancestral Profession

Distance between Apu and Mother grows

72. Apu at exams. The routine of work, studies and friends continues	Apu's new pattern is settled. Mother and her ideas recede in the background.
73. Letter from Sarbojaya pleading him to visit	
74. Apu answers in the negative	Contrast to the first letter from Apu.

Sarbojaya Ill and Alone, Apu away, She Succumbs

75. Disappointment of Apu's letter, neighbour woman talks of Apu's marriage	Repetition of distraction with the negative letter when the Baul came at her door in Nischindipur (PP 28).
76. Apu at Calcutta, his misjudgement	Apu's new life has its own worries, his misjudgment spells misery later.
77.Sarbojaya ill, hallucinates Apu, collapses	Nirupama tries to help, but Sarbojaya strong in her resolve that Apu should come on his own and he does not. Moment of Director's privilege. Extension of the sad feelings
	The death is not shown, it hits Apu badly. It precipitates his decision to give up the family profession. He regarded mother as the difficult block in following the new life that had opened for him.

Apu Severes Bonds with Ancestral Profession

78. Apu receives letter about mother's illness, rushes home on the train, oblivious of the balmseller	Height of anxiety for Apu.
79. Apu rushes home, finds Bhabtaran instead and knows. He mourns.	Apu's search for mother as he moves in all directions :Visual reminder of his movement in confusion in the tall grass where he had lost his way He had not paid heed to mother's urgent appeal for a visit and he regrets it. Reminder of Sarbojaya's rejection of Indir on her last visit to the house and her wordless reaction after her death

80.Apu and Bhabataran: Bhabataran consoles and advises, Apu declines, Apu leaves Manasapota with mother's belongings, barefoot on his way to the station.	Bhabataran's words have no effect. He does not even touch his feet or observe other polite norms. He simply breaks away from the bond of tradition.
	With new education, Apu severs his bonds with the family profession completely by the end of Aparajito, even in a situation when he has not a good alternative worked out for himself.

From temporary absence in Nischindipur we move to abandonment of the ancestral village. From the bigger town like Benaras we move again to a small village and then again to the big city. With every move there is a decimation of the family and snapping of old bonds.

APUR SANSAR

Prologue

Apu receives a testimonial from his professor	Apu could not complete his education beyond the two years of college.
The Professor advises him to take up writing as a profession	His talent for writing is acknowledged.
Apu takes his leave as a procession passes by.	Apu has to start a life of an unemployed educated person.
	The prologue serves to link Aparajito with Apur Sansar. Apu is now around 20 plus age.

Apu's Life in Isolation

Apu and his Calcutta Surroundings

1.Rainy morning. Apu asleep. The ink stained chadar. Apu drenches and enjoys the rain	The next morning sequence in AS 32 will be done in terms of Apu's prank in the life of togetherness with Aparna. The hooting of the engine whistle, the noise of the yard, the inadequacy of the tap water supply are aspects of this physical environment which is a variation in terms of the shift of location.

2. Apu and the landlord who demands rent arrears	Apu's isolation and difficulties as he struggles to survive in a new mode of living in Calcutta. He has to find devices of dodging the houseowner and delay payments. The electric light is a variation for expressing Apu's irritation with the houseowner a playful manner. The first social interaction is a nagging economic pressure, the rent arrears for three months and a threat of losing the room.
3.Apu's namesake neighbour who hands him over a letter delivered to him by mistake	Another aspect of social interactions is Apu's bachelor status and the women of the building who turn heads away as he passes.
	The opening sequence lays the pattern of life for Apu in isolation, in the noisy physical environment, with absence of any cordiality in social relations The strain appears in the books he takes out for selling to pay the rent arrears. The neighbour (Apu's namesake) interacts over the publisher's letter delivered to him by mistake. He mentions girl friends and advises to keep away from marriage as long as possible. Clearly, the norms of interaction have loosened but people in immediate environment are not close. However, Apu's enthusiasm and optimism continues.

Apu fails to find a job

4. Apu at a primary school. He is rejected because he is overqualified	Contrast with Apu's own ambition not to be tied up with a job and be free to write (AS 17).
5. Apu at a bottle labelling shop. He is repulsed by the working conditions	Contrast with Apu's aspiration, similar to Harihar's dream of settling down as a writer of new plays and poetry (PP 8 & 9).
6.Apu on his way home, frustrated, seeking solace in the publisher's letter and music, avoids girl in the next building	Contrast with the girl in the next building who wants to attract Apu. She seems to have continued even after Apu's marriage as Aparna mentions her in the letter (AS 42). In PP Durga escapes in her child's world when threatened (PP 2). Apu escapes into his private world of the publisher's letter and playing flute.
	The stress of living accosts the educated unemployed Apu as he seeks means of survival in the big city.

Pulu finds Apu

7.Pulu knocks the door, enters and old friends meet after a long gap.	A special relationship with this friend is introduced.
8. Pulu talks about the efforts he took to find his address.	The intensity of feeling underlined.
9. They decide to go out. Apu promises him a meal of potato and rice some day.	Apu's low status is not a barrier in their friendship.
	Pulu plays the vital role of pulling Apu out of his isolation twice in the film. In this segment he does it for the first time and repeats in AS 67-69.

Pulu Connects with Apu

Pulu and Apu at the restaurant

10. They compare notes.	Contrast with the direct manner in which Pulu approaches Apu the second time in AS 67-69.
11. Pulu inquires about his job, his skill of typing, the possibility of a job.	In AS 27 While consenting to marry Aparna Apu confirms with Pulu that a job will be arranged for him. Apu is seen later with a job as a typist (AS 40).
12.Pulu asks about the railway job. Apu did not take it because that was against workers on strike	Simple human approach of Apu revealed, though he is not actively political.
	The quality of their friendship emphasised through this and the next sequence

Pulu and Apu: invitation to attend a marriage in the family.

13.Pulu makes the suggestion	Simple human approach of Apu revealed, though he is not actively political.
14.Apu resists, Pulu gives a tempting description of the countryside	Pulu knows what Apu likes and makes his invitation more attractive.
15.Apu agrees	Friends can easily be included in family events.

Pulu and Apu : After the Play

16. Apu recites a poem loudly. A policeman calls. They escape shouting about their identities from the mythological stories	After good food and good entertainment, Apu continues to have a bit of playful mischief.
17.Apu refuses the idea of taking a job because he wants to be free to write.	The novel figures in his conversation with Aparna (AS 36) and in his lonely wandering in AS 63.
	Pulu as a friend is heartily free and open. The old strands of earlier days are quickly picked up without any awkwardness. Pulu is a practical, successful man. Yet he cares for Apu's creativity and at the same time wants him to be comfortably placed in life. The relationship of this pair of friends is similar to Ranu and Durga in PP.

Apu's Marriage

On The River to Khulna

18. The countryside on the banks of the river.Apu plays the flute	Apu's flute repeats from AS 6 will recur in AS 32. He plays the tune of the Tagore song : Aamaar Shonaar Banglaa /Aami Tomaar Bhaalo Bashii (My Golden Bangal/I love thee) The open river landscape provides a romantic ambience for Apu's mind.
19. Apu recites a Tagore poem	Apu has been good at recitation. (APJT 39).
20. Pulu reads Apu's novel and congratulates him	Pulu's appreciation here contrasts with his admonition (AS 68-69).

The arranged marriage called off

21.Preparations	Reaction of Aparna's mother to Apu has adulation similar to expressed at the time of Apu's birth (PP 6). The importance of the male child plays an important role in shaping of Apu's personal sense of self. Later, Aparna too would nourish it (AS 36).
22.The arrival of the bridegroom and the fiasco	The bandplayers show similarity in modes of celebration (PP 29). The bridegroom tumbles out of the palanquin, it is impossible to cover his condition. Contrast with Apu as bridegroom (AS 27).
23. Aparna's mother refuses to agree to this marriage.	Protective function of the mother as powerful aspect of bringing up of the girl child.

Apu gets married

24.The crisis in the family: finding another bridegroom	The felt intensity of this crisis is similar to the crisis of survival, but it operates within the frame of beliefs in astrological implications of a broken marriage arrangement.
25.Apu approached with a proposal	Elders help in persuading Apu. Elders intervene with Harihar as well, ineffectively (PP 38).
26. Apu's reservations and consent	In the process of finding himself as a substitute bridegroom. Apu questions the suggestion itself, but is drawn in by the idea of a noble deed. His sense of doing a noble deed goes back to throwing away the stolen necklace (PP 42).
	This is a sudden turn in the narrative, based on the chance presence of Apu as an eligible bachelor who could save the honour of the family and the girl's fate. It is firmly based in the structure of superstitions around marriage and it is the act of assertion on the part of Aparna's mother that Aparna is saved from the possibility of marriage with an insane groom.

Apu's Life in Togetherness

Apu and Aparna: Trust and Transparency

27. Apu anxious in the bridal chamber, establishes rapport with Aparna	Apu begins the relationship with a need to share and ensure mutual consent.
28.Apu tells Aparna about his condition and checks what she knows and whether she is ready to enter a life with him under poor conditions. Aparna agrees	
29.Apu relaxed, decides to take her to Calcutta	Aparna's willingness matches his way of thinking.
	The boatman's song will recur in the scene of his first meeting with Kajal (AS 71). The basic bond has been established.

Apu and Aparna : Confidence and Mutuality

30. Apu and Aparna in the Calcutta room; Apu connects with the neighbours	Delicate Aparna as a contrast to the stark surrounding. Admiration from neighbours, variation in response when Apu was a bachelor and now that he is married.
31. Apu tries to get a servant, Aparna prevents such expense	Apu's prank with the tied knot introduces the playfulness in their relationship. Aparna emphasises the value of their togetherness more than money.
32. Aparna's prank with the paper bag	Aparna matches the playfulness with a prank. Mealtime made happy by mutual fanning.
	The confidence of living together happily is designed by showing mutual sensitivity and an effort to complement each other.

Apu and Aparna : Fun and Maturity

33.Aparna delays going to bed	Aparna learns English: Her effort to reach up to Apu.
34.Apu and Aparna at the cinema hall	The city entertainment at the end of range of forms of entertainment. Recall the village entertainments.
35. The ride home in horse carriage	The talk about dedicating the novel to 'Wife' contrasts when the pages are scattered in wilderness (AS 63). The name Kajal rings in AS 64 when Pulu talks of Kajal.
	Apu's world of togetherness is a dream world. In contrast to the earlier generation of Harihar and Sarbojaya and many of his own generation (AS 41), he discovers ways of belonging which generate a quality of sustenance in the relationship of marriage. It is open, mutual and articulate, it has greater fun and sense of humour

Apu While Aparna is Away

Aparna's Departure

36.Murari and Aparna in the train compartment	The railway and parting repeated. Compositionally the distance between them grows through the scene.
37.Apu and Aparna wordless. The train starts and Aparna breaks into a spate of instructions	The pent up quality of the pain of separation and a last moment release in practical trivia.

38. The train leaves, Apu left alone	Details of the train. The railway functions to separate Apu from his dear ones, first in APJT 56 and now in AS 39. The jewellery mentioned here will be delivered to Aparna's father when Apu decides to leave without Kajal (AS 79).

Aparna's letter

39. Apu at work reminisces about Aparna	
40. His colleague notices his happiness	
41.Apu reads Aparna's letter.	Aparna has filled Apu's life in a manner that her presence is continued by Apu's involvement in her letters.

Colleague and Apu

42. Colleague talks about Apu's happiness	Aparna has filled Apu's life in a manner that her presence is continued by Apu's involvement in her letters.
43. He talks about his ever-obedient wife	The other side of bringing up the girl child to be obedient, something which Durga resisted.
44. Apu reads the letter on his way home	
	Apu's actual experience of togetherness in marriage is in sharp contrast to the suggestion of postponing marriage as much as possible (AS 3) and the colleague's complaint about the ever-obedient wife (AS 44)

Apu's Grief

Murari Brings Bad News

45. As Apu returns from work, he finds Murari waiting at the door	Aparna has filled Apu's life in a manner that her presence is continued by Apu's involvement in her letters.
46. Murari falteringly tells about Aparna's death	Aparna has filled Apu's life in a manner that her presence is continued by Apu's involvement in her letters.
47. Apu violently hits Murari and collapses.	Uncontrolled violence by Apu himself.
	The shortlived phase of marital happiness comes to a sudden end and knocks Apu flat.

Apu lost in grief

48.Apu in bed, lies tearless	This silent suffering continues till Apu meets Pulu (AS69). It contrasts with the immediate violent reaction of hitting Murari.
49.Neighbour woman comes in	Distraction by a chattering presence. Repetition of situation from APJT 76. The difference in the way Apu regards marriage and the general social customary attitude.
50.Apu gets up with difficulty, reflected in the mirror	The mirror images of Apu shaving (AS 3) Aparna grooming (AS 33) and Apu in grief reflect variations in the use of the mirror image in the Trilogy.

Apu writes to Pulu and leaves Calcutta

51. Apu near the railway tracks, in despair	The suicidal thoughts and the vicinity of the tracks provide another aspect of railways in the design.
52. A pig hurt by the engine	Animal live in close contact with human beings.
53.Apu writes to Pulu	Writing is a recurrent motif in the Trilogy.
	The movement from thc happy world of togetherness (AS 31 to 39) to absolute social and mental isolation here is complete.

Apu Wanders in Isolation

Apu on train

54.Apu at a window, as the train rushes away speedily	Apu is restless.The trains moving in opposite directions reflect the effort to run away as speedily as one possibly can.
55.Aparna's baby in cradle	Similarity to Apu in cradle (PP 7 & 9)
56. Aparna's mother heaves a sigh and sobs	Contrast with Indir singing a lullaby for Apu in cradle (PP 7 & 9)
	The segment serves dual function of the narration of what happens to the baby and the emotional quality of Apu's grief. Constant change of location does not free him from pain.

Apu on Seashore

57.Apu now with a beard on the seashore	
58. Apu watches the waves	
59. The waves wash away the marks on the sand	The vast expanse of the seashore and the massive waves run parallel to the continuous waves of grief and sorrow. Ripples of water composed with a human character is a motif used extensively in the Trilogy.

	This segment indicates passage of time, Apu's intensified renunciation.

Apu consigns the novel to wilderness

60. Apu wandering aimlessly through a forest.	
61.Apu at dawn, goes up a hill, takes out the manuscript	The importance of dawn in many scenes in the Trilogy. Music here important, a dignified simplicity based on the notes of the Apu theme in the Title Music.
62. He throws the pages to the wind, watches as they scatter and are taken away by the wind	
	Apu disconnects with his own creative writing . The feeling of renunciation and meaninglessness of life reach a climax here. The movement of the world of togetherness (AS 31 to 39)to complete social and mental isolation ends here.

Pulu Reconnects with Apu
Kajal, Apu's son, is now six

63.Kajal with a mask and sling	Kajal (without parental cover) is aggressive rather than playful. He is confused and therefore misunderstood. In PP the children's world was well created within the adult world. In APJT it develops to a search for independence. In AS it gets completely isolated. Kajal grows up without the duplex of protection and correction from parents, as also from a community that shares norms of good behaviour.
64.Pulu back from abroad, learns about Apu's total neglect of the child	Pulu had received the letter Apu had posted before he left Calcutta on his wanderings. Kajal is a confused child carrying an idea of what a father is like. Grandfather takes an authoritative, critical and sarcastic attitude in the matter. This creates a very tense triangle of tension between Grandfather, and Kajal and the absent Apu.
65. Pulu takes Apu's address from his uncle	
	Pulu's role as a friend takes on a deeper shade and initiates Apu's return to family responsibility. Pulu is acting not merely as a friend in need but a friend who would prompt a person to do the right thing irrespective of circumstances.

Index of MUSIC

Music in the Trilogy forms an element of design. Music touches the inner structure of feelings embodied in a narrative scene by contributing to the intensity and quality of feeling of the scene. This layer of feeling which cannot be reached by the filmic audio-visual composition is stimulated by background music (and also sometimes by silence).

Take an example. The PP Theme Tune is used in APJT when Sarbojaya is leaving Benaras on way to Manasapota. As the train enters the landscape of Bengal, PP Theme music comes on . Sarbojaya has a faint smile of relief. Here the Theme Tune takes on the feeling of security generated by the familiar landscape, since Sarbojaya was always bothered by the unfamiliarity, the tensed-up quality of the Benares environment as she experienced it. In AS, when Apu narrates the story of the novel to Pulu the PP Theme tune is in the background. Here The Tune takes on the entire quality of the village ethos in which Apu grew up as a child.

We have always tried to refer to music in the main text of this book. Here are some additional notes on music in the Trilogy.

Pather Panchali

The Pather Panchali Theme Tune goes as follows: (Bold typeface like Sa indicates higher octave)

Pa Dha Saaaa / Ni Pa Dhaaaa
PaDha Pa Saaaa / Ni Pa Dhaaaa
Ma Dha Paaaa / Ga Pa Maaaa
RePa MaPa Gaaaa /Sa Reeee Saaaa

The main text of the book has details of where the PP Theme Tune occurs in the film apart from the credit titles of and at the end title. In the body of the film it occurs nine times, on each occasion some event of importance is happening. The Tune also gets into APJT twice and once in AS. In the design sense, the PP Theme Tune acts as binding device of the Trilogy.

In addition,Indir's song occurs in the film four times, most remarkably sung in her own voice on her funeral sequence. Indir's anger is accompanied by a single note vibrato. Drums are prominent with respect to Durga's punishment for the theft of beads. The drums repeat on Apu as he discovers the stolen beads and decides to throw them in the pond to keep the sister's secret. Drums also signal the presence of the goddess Durga. Happpy tunes occur several times in the film. The rain sequence has a piece in Rag Desh. A sitar piece in Rag Todi follows the sequence following Durga's death.

The piece of music which replaces Sarbojaya's crying is named by us as Mother's Wail. It is a piece in Rag Patdeep in the highest octave played on tarshnai. The shape of Mother's Wail is as follows: (Italics bold typeface as Pa indicates flat, komal note.)

Pa Ni Sa Re Gaaa / Ga Ma Pa Gaa / Ga Ma Pa Ma Pa Ga / Ree SaRe Ni Sa /
Ga Ma Paaaa / Ga Ma Pa Niiii / Niiii Dha Pa Ma Ga /
Ga Ma Pa Ni Saaaa / Ni Sa Dhaaa Paaa Maaa Gaaa/
Ma Ga Ree SaRe NiSaaa

Mother's Wail : The last two lines of the above sargam recur on the fleeting segment when Kajal runs upto Apu at the end of Apur Sansar.

Aparajito

The Title Music of Aparajito has the following sargam

Sa Ma Pa Dha Pa Ma / Ma Pa Ga Re Sa

SaMa PaDha PaDha MaPa GaRe Saa

The high musical notes at Harihar's Death have the following sargam of Rag Jog.

Sa Ni Ni Pa / Ni Pa Ma Ga / Ma Ga Ga Saaaaa

Harihar's Death Theme recurs twice in Aparajito, and once in Apur Sansar. The details are in the main text of the book. In addition musical passages of different kinds, sometimes based on the Apu Theme derived from the Title sargam occur in Aparaito. Satyajit Ray felt that Aparajito needed more music.

Apur Sansar

The Title Music of Apur Sansar has the following sargams.

Sa Sa Re Ga / SaRe GaSaaa /
Ga Ma Ga Sa / ReGa ReSaaa /
Sa Sa Re Ga / ReGa SaReee /
Ga Ma Ga Sa / ReGa ReSaaa /
Pa Pa Ma Ma / MaPa MaGa Gaaa /
Sa Sa Ree / ReMa GaSaaa /

This also includes the segment of the Apu Theme which is repeated several times in the film in several variations played in different speeds and on different instruments, notably in the forest scene leading to the sunrise on the hilltop when Apu casts away the pages of his novel in a final gesture of renunciation. The music here scored for flute and strings, has, as Satyajit Ray puts it, "the noble simplicity of a vedic hymn."